T0118486

THE MAGIC OF MONDAY

A Fable about the Winning Formula
for Career Success

OBI ABUCHI

iUniverse, Inc.
Bloomington

The Magic of Monday
A Fable about the Winning Formula for Career Success

Copyright © 2012 by Obi Abuchi

All rights reserved. No part of this book may be used or reproduced by any means, graphic, electronic, or mechanical, including photocopying, recording, taping or by any information storage retrieval system without the written permission of the publisher except in the case of brief quotations embodied in critical articles and reviews.

iUniverse books may be ordered through booksellers or by contacting:

iUniverse
1663 Liberty Drive
Bloomington, IN 47403
www.iuniverse.com
1-800-Authors (1-800-288-4677)

Because of the dynamic nature of the Internet, any web addresses or links contained in this book may have changed since publication and may no longer be valid. The views expressed in this work are solely those of the author and do not necessarily reflect the views of the publisher, and the publisher hereby disclaims any responsibility for them.

Any people depicted in stock imagery provided by Thinkstock are models, and such images are being used for illustrative purposes only.

Certain stock imagery © Thinkstock.

ISBN: 978-1-4759-5099-1 (sc)
ISBN: 978-1-4759-5101-1 (e)
ISBN: 978-1-4759-5100-4 (dj)

Library of Congress Control Number: 2012917495

Printed in the United States of America

iUniverse rev. date: 10/11/2012

To Peju, my queen and princess all rolled into one.

And to my little champions, Lemar, Zikora, and Kobi. May you always have a winning attitude and winning focus!

Contents

Foreword

Young people today are faced with a bewildering array of choices, opportunities, and pressures in education and their professional lives. Compared to their parents' generation, they will spend much longer in the workplace. So discovering what they enjoy and where their real talents lie early on, and realising that it won't be fun all the time, especially when they start out, are valuable lessons best learnt quickly.

It is often said that 'experience teaches,' and we learn a lot in life from making our own mistakes. As you'll see from Josh's story in this highly enjoyable and valuable read, part of the value of mentoring is avoiding doing things wrong in the first place by learning from someone else's mistakes!

I have always believed that good mentoring is vital for good business. Responsible business leaders should nurture future talent and recognise that young, innovative voices can reinvigorate the CEO's occasionally jaded take on life. Equally, it can often be that by helping to develop another's abilities, we learn more about where our own strengths lie, and mutually rewarding friendships can grow.

To me, this book is a great distillation of key skills and an array of accumulated business knowledge in a very accessible and engaging format. It will speak clearly to an audience of young people forming their professional behaviours and hopefully put them on the road to career success! It's also for people with their feet on the lower rungs of the corporate ladder who are wondering how they will ever get to the top and those young professionals simply looking to develop their career prospects.

So much of what Josh learns in this book are lessons that I have learnt myself in my years in business and would eagerly pass on to the younger generation.

Stephen Howard, CEO, Business in the Community

Acknowledgements

They say it takes more than one person to write a book. Well, in my case, that's definitely true. As a matter of fact, as I explain in the introduction, it took just more than seventy-five people to write this book.

I'm grateful to all those executives, business leaders, and managers who gave of their time to share lessons and insights that they believed would help and inspire the next generation to excel in whatever career or vocation they choose.

So here's a big thank you to Andrew Agerbak, Kriss Akabusi, Sonita Alleyne, Ismail Amla, Peter Ashwell, Julie Bardouille, Laurence Barrett, Paul Bateman, Angela Bentley, Nicola Blatch, Lynne Brooke, Mike Butler, Mark Campbell, Rachel Campbell, René Carayol, Wendy Cartwright, Michael Cassidy CBE, Mark Clarke, Patrick Clarke, Julia Cleverdon CVO CBE, Andy Cole, Daniel Coulton, Gregory Cousland, Ken Dalton, Arvinder Dhesi, Susan Dowling, Steven D'Souza, Jo Dunne, Paul

Dyer, Mike Evans, Toby Foggo, Juliette Foster, Richard Garner, P-Y Gerbeau, Carolyn Gray, Laura Haynes, Katrin Hentszel, Bill Hester, David Hopley, Phil Hullah, Aye Idehen, Richie Dayo Johnson, Ian Joseph, Sir Paul Judge, David Kaner, Dwight Lawrence, Nevil Lee, Martyn Lewis CBE, Christine Lloyd, Frank Makan, George Metcalfe, Julie Meyer, Jon Millidge, Paul Milliken, Sir Mark Moody-Stuart, Terry Morgan, Bill Murphy, Steve Norris, Stephen O'Brien CBE, Bola Ogun, David Oliver, Rupert Pennant-Rea, Vikas Pota, Barry Quirk CBE, Amanda Rigby, Martin Saurma-Jeltsch, Mark Shann, Ian Smith, Brian Thomas, Dr Koyi Ugboma, Dr George Watkins CBE, Ben Whitworth, Steve Wiggins, Peter Williams, Stephen Williams, Rob Wye, and the mysterious you-know-who.

Introduction

We're at a point in history when competition for jobs is fiercer than ever; unemployment levels are extremely worrying, even for those in employment; and the concept of a 'job for life' is no longer the norm. This reality is a challenge for millions of young people and young professionals with a desire to secure work, advance their career, or simply rediscover their career ambitions and go on to achieve career success.

If you have only recently embarked on your career journey or are getting ready to, then what you are about to read in this book will undoubtedly shape or forever change your view of what it takes to succeed in your career. For other young professionals, the ideas will empower you to take your career to the next level.

The late Steve Jobs said, 'You can't connect the dots looking forward; you can only connect them looking backwards.' When it comes to our working lives, connecting the dots of life can be a huge challenge, especially for young people and many young professionals. That is why learning from people in the know—those with experience who have gone and, in some cases, crashed before us—can be priceless.

Numerous business leaders, senior executives, and managers from a variety of organisations and industries have contributed to the ideas within this book. All of these individuals, tried and tested in their own way, share a particular passion of mine: inspiring and enabling young professionals and young people to tap into their full potential and go beyond what they perceive as the limits of their capabilities.

As a token of my appreciation and gratitude to their generosity (both in terms of time and wisdom), I have taken on the challenge of passing on their tried and tested ideas, insight, and wisdom.

Let me backtrack a little and tell you exactly how this book came about, its structure, and what you can expect from it.

Over a seven-month period spanning from 2007 to 2008, I interviewed seventy-five experienced professionals as part of what I called 'Project 75.' I asked them all the same set of research questions with the sole aim of trying to find out critical lessons and success principles that could be passed on to others, especially those of the younger generation.

I didn't actually start out with plans to write a book, but the ideas and insights coming out of the interviews were so rich that I felt compelled to turn this into a book and share the ideas more widely.

One executive, who at the time of the interview was the chief financial officer for an educational charity, described how she often tells her daughter, 'Try and learn from others and their mistakes rather than waste time, sometimes years, learning from your own.' Ignoring the fact that her daughter was only five then, you've got to admit that that is great advice.

This book, among other things, is an opportunity to learn from both the victories and mistakes of others. Personally, if I had a fiver for every minute I've wasted making mistakes, mistakes that could have easily been avoided … Well, let's just say, 'Step aside, Richard Branson!'

As you can appreciate, there are so many different ways to write a book. So, in putting this together, I thought about the best way to distil and communicate all of the excellent advice, ideas, insight, and principles that I had picked up, directly and indirectly, from the victories and failures of those I had interviewed. I wondered, *What would happen if I could create a virtual 'school of life' that allows the reader to vicariously network with and learn from all those I have spoken to? How would they respond to and benefit from such an opportunity?*

It then dawned on me that some of the best books I've read have used stories to communicate simple and valuable truths—from Paulo Coelho's *The Alchemist* to the Bible. And that's when I decided I would tell a story and invite readers to come on a journey with the fictional Josh, a young professional who struggles in his career and encounters several mentors along the way.

What lessons will he learn? What will he learn about himself? What impact will it have on his career, his life, his attitude, and his focus? Would any of it really make a difference?

As you go on this journey with Josh and other characters, I am convinced that the real, condensed insight of more than seventy-five seasoned professionals, and a few insights of my own, will challenge your thinking, engage your mind, and inspire you to fulfil your full potential in what is now a small, global marketplace.

At the end of each chapter, you will find a summary of the key principles and success lessons that Josh has picked up, which you can use as an aide-memoire for yourself.

Above all, you will discover the winning formula for career success. Apply it and watch the magic unfold in your career.

Here's to maximising *your* true potential.

Prologue: A Noble Aspiration

No one got to where he or she is
without first starting where he or she did.

—Anonymous

The floor was littered with scrunched-up pieces of paper.
It had taken quite a long time to get it right, but Josh felt
happy as he read through the letter. He reached over for
a brown envelope, folded the sheet, and tucked it into the
envelope.

'What are you doing, Josh?' His mother had just walked
into the room and seemed amused.

'I'm writing a letter to Mrs Havier.'

'Awww. I'm sure she'll be happy that you've written as
promised.' She paused, looked around the room, and then
said, 'What's all this mess though?'

'Er …' He suddenly noticed how much paper he had wasted while writing his letter. 'I kept getting it wrong, but it's OK now. Could you post it for me?'

'Sure. What did you write about?' she asked.

'Well, I wrote about my new school and about that film … Actually, would you like to read it?' He was slowly pulling the letter out of the envelope.

His mother nodded, took the letter, and unfolded it to read.

Dear Mrs Havier,

I really miss being in your class and miss all my friends too. I am starting to enjoy my new school, though sometimes the kids in my class laugh at me when I'm reading. I think they find my accent funny. It used to make me sad, but now I just make jokes and laugh about it too, so it doesn't make me feel so sad anymore.

I think you'll be pleased to hear that I now know what I want to be when I grow up. Leesa and I recently watched a movie about a doctor who makes people look better after they've been in an accident. Leesa said he was a plastic surgeon. That really is a strange name, but he was really good and helped lots of people. So that's what I want to be when I grow up.

I think I'd like to be one of the best doctors in the world. I could even be the first doctor in the world to find the cure for cancer, because it's very bad and Mummy says the doctors are still trying to find a cure so that no one will have to die from it like Daddy did. She said if I'm good, she'll buy me a special junior doctor's kit for my tenth birthday next month. I can't wait.

I've got to go now. Please say hello to Roy, Berhan, and Julie for me. Mum and Leesa send their love.

Bye for now.

Josh

'That looks great.' She grinned and stroked Josh's head. 'I'm sure you'll be a great doctor.'

He broke into a huge smile.

'I'll get a stamp for you to put on the envelope, and then I'll post it for you on my way to work on Monday,' said Josh's mum. 'While I'm getting the stamp, please tidy up the mess. It'll be lunchtime soon.'

'Thanks, Mum. I will.'

***

A few weeks later, Josh received a reply from Mrs Havier. He smiled as he read it. She was really happy to receive Josh's letter and learn that he was settling into his new school, and she mentioned that all of his friends missed him too. As for becoming a doctor, she had no doubt that he would indeed make a fine doctor someday.

1—Get Back in the Driver's Seat

Character—the willingness to accept responsibility for one's own life—is the source from which self-respect springs.

—Joan Didion

He entered his flat, kicked off his shoes, and collapsed on the sofa. He was exhausted. It had been another extremely long day.

'Talk about no rest for the wicked,' he muttered to himself.

Monday had never been Josh's favourite day, and the weekly 7 a.m. briefing certainly wasn't his ideal way to start the week. The creatives, who designed the marketing campaigns, had been in even earlier, fussing about a new campaign that was being launched this week, and when he arrived, hardly anybody spoke to him.

The family-owned advertising company had only thirty-five employees, but with a big reputation and loyal customers, it regularly punched well above its weight. Most of the day-to-day operations were overseen by Pete, the older son of Mick Teveo, the founding director, whom everyone referred to as 'the big boss.' Even Pete called him that, much to everyone's amusement.

With the end of his six-month probation drawing near, and knowing that he was struggling to meet performance expectations, Josh didn't feel too optimistic that they would keep him on, even if Pete was a good friend of his older sister, Leesa.

As a marketing assistant, it was his job to carry out research in support of various marketing campaigns. He knew it was unrealistic to expect to be responsible for the development of an actual marketing strategy at this stage, but he had hoped that by now he would be doing more than market research and organising the distribution of promotional literature.

It didn't help that he had a strained relationship with Lewis, his manager. As far as Josh was concerned, Lewis didn't like him. He was always going on about Josh's poor attitude, but Josh felt he was far too strict about doing things right, giving him no room to exercise his own creativity. Considering that he was at least a foot and a half taller than Lewis, Josh convinced himself that Lewis was simply suffering from small-man syndrome. He was certain that Lewis would have fired him already if not for Pete.

He recently moaned to a colleague about Lewis. 'He should try doing the market research for a change! I always get the boring stuff, and yet all he does is complain about my lack of urgency.'

It was typical for staff at the company to put in an extra fifteen to twenty hours a week, especially when they had deadlines on major projects. Josh hated working to deadlines. Although they all got paid for working overtime, the busy weeks felt like they were every week.

As he lay on the sofa, he couldn't help but think that, at twenty-seven, this wasn't what he expected his life to be like. He wondered where it had all gone wrong. Nine years earlier, though it seemed like only yesterday, he was hoping to fulfil his ambition of going to one of the best universities in the world to study medicine. He wanted his work to make a difference, but now he felt he was simply working just to get by. And he hated it.

However, each time he thought about the number of jobs he'd had over the last six years—since graduating from university with a degree in physics and management—he was determined to make this job work. Sometimes, he felt that had more to do with not wanting to disappoint his mum, Leesa, or even Pete.

He could sense the sinking feeling in his stomach when suddenly the jingling of keys in the front door caught his attention.

It had to be Paul, one of Josh's flatmates. He taught science at a private school and organised an after-school club, so he rarely got home before 8 p.m. on weekdays. Tim, their other flatmate, was currently in Dubai. He worked for a management consultancy and was often out of town for a few weeks at a time. He earned a very good salary and paid his share of the rent in advance, three months at a time. Josh felt so envious of him.

'Hey, how's it going?' said Paul casually as he dropped his keys by the door and headed towards the kitchen.

'I'm cool,' replied Josh.

Paul shouted from the kitchen, 'Are we still heading out to watch the game?'

'Oh, yeah. I forgot about that. It's been a mad day at work, to be honest. I hardly had time to breathe.'

'That great, eh?'

'A pretty rubbish day, actually,' Josh mumbled as he walked towards the kitchen and stood right outside the door. 'Do you ever feel like you're living someone else's life?'

'Huh?' replied Paul. He was pouring some juice into a glass and not looking at Josh.

'You know what I mean. Clocking in and out every day, answering to a difficult boss, going through the motions, doing a job that just doesn't feel like it was ever meant to be for you.'

'Oh, here we go again,' said Paul as he rolled his eyes. 'Er ... I guess. Although somehow I've always known what I wanted to do and just gone after it, even though it wasn't what Mum and Dad wanted me to do. I don't know. Maybe I'm lucky, but I really love my work.'

'Well, of course you would. They've got great facilities in your school, plus you earn good dosh, you get to organise regular science trips, and you even have free lunches. Please! Who wouldn't love that?'

'That's true,' he said as he smiled. 'But, hey, those are just perks. I love teaching. There's no question that it's hard work, and those kids can be a real pain in the neck sometimes. But I honestly think I'd enjoy teaching anywhere, perks or not.'

'Lucky you,' said Josh as he sighed. 'Most of the time I just feel empty at work. Somehow, I know I could be doing so much more with my life, but I'm just not sure what more is. Right now, I have zero passion for what I do. Zilch! Nada! And it doesn't help that I always get the boring stuff to do at work.'

'I think you're taking this all too seriously, J. Come on! There's more to life than work.'

Josh just glared at Paul in response.

Obi Abuchi

'Whoa! If eyes could kill …' said Paul, looking away. 'By the way, I thought you were excited about this job when you got it? It's been what, four or five months?'

Josh rubbed his head. 'Almost six!' he replied. 'Maybe I wasn't meant to be doing this. I'm in the business of helping others communicate their ideas, and I don't even know what's really going on in my own head. What irony. Is it really possible to do something you love and almost not know the difference between work and play?'

'Well …' began Paul.

'Hey, you know what? Forget I even brought this up. You're probably right. Maybe I take this all too seriously. Let's get outta here. Otherwise, we might not even catch the end of the game.'

'Great. I was beginning to think I'd have to listen to you whinge all evening. By the way, you'll never guess what we had for lunch at school today.'

'Hey!' Josh landed a punch on Paul's shoulder.

'Oww! Just kidding. Lighten up!'

They grabbed their keys and jackets and headed out the door.

***

6

A few days later, Josh had just arrived in the office when his mobile phone rang. It was Paul.

'Hi, mate,' Paul said. 'You know what? I've been thinking. If you're really serious about figuring out this career dilemma of yours, I know someone who might be able to help. He's a good friend of my dad and is also my godfather. His name is Tomas Woodes. I'm not sure if I've mentioned him before, but he was instrumental in helping my dad come to terms with the fact that I didn't want to be part of his law firm and that I could still excel in a different field.'

'Oh. I didn't know that. He sounds like one of those life coaches.'

'Not really. He runs a private equity company called TW Capital, and he's also a guest lecturer on an MBA programme for some business school in Europe. I don't remember which. Anyway, as you can imagine, he's extremely busy, but I think he might be able to help. I sent him a couple of emails, and he's responded to say he doesn't mind your getting in touch. He's currently out of town, but he'll be back at the end of the week and knows to expect your call.'

'Wow. Really? And you're sure he's happy for me to get in touch?'

'Well, it took a little bit of convincing, but he's definitely happy for you to call him.'

'OK. Cool. Thanks a mill. Wait a second, what do you mean by a little bit of convincing?'

'Don't worry. Like I said, he's extremely busy, but he's a good friend of the family so it's cool.'

'OK. Nice one. You know, that's the first thing that's made me smile all morning. Thanks.'

'No worries. I hope your smile lasts longer than this morning. This isn't the first time you've moaned about your job, so I figured it's about time you made some real headway.'

'Well, let's see.'

'By the way, don't forget that you and Tim are invited to the charity event that Jaz is organising on Saturday evening. It's a black-tie event, so remember to pick up a tux. I've just sent Tim a text. He's back on Friday night.'

Jasmine, Paul's fiancée, was the events and hospitality manager for a chain of Marriott hotels. Quite the sports fanatic, she had only just come back from taking part in a charity challenge in South America and had raised over five thousand pounds for the hotel's charity. And now she was organising its annual charity gala. Paul and Jaz were planning on getting married the following year, with Josh as best man.

'Oh, yeah. Thanks for the reminder.'

'Cool. Anyway, gotta go. My kids arrive soon.'

***

A week went by before Josh finally made the call to Mr Woodes. He tried his mobile number, and it went to voicemail; he decided not to leave a message. Paul had also given him a work number, so he tried that and got through to Mr Woodes's PA, Sheree. After he explained who he was, she told him that Tomas was out of town on an overnight business trip but he would return the call the next day when he was back in the office.

Like that's going to happen, Josh thought.

He left his number anyway.

The next day was Friday. At around four o'clock in the afternoon, Josh got a phone call from a private number. When he picked up the phone, it was Mr Woodes.

Sounding rather surprised, he said, 'Oh. Hi. Thanks for calling me back, Mr Woodes.'

'That's no problem at all. By the way, you can call me Tomas.'

'OK. Tomas it is.'

'Paul told me about your situation. Something about a career crisis?'

'Yeah. Something like that. He said it might be worth having a chat with you.'

'I'm certainly happy to see what I can do. Here's what I suggest. I did have a lunch appointment next week Friday that has just cancelled, so I've now got thirty minutes free over lunch before I have to head off to the airport for an afternoon flight to France. Would 12.30 work for you here at my office?'

Tomas described where his office building was.

Josh usually took only a thirty-minute lunch break, but Mr Woodes's office was fortunately less than a five-minute walk away from his own, so an hour or so for lunch would be fine. Besides, he figured, this was a busy man doing him a favour.

'Yes, that's great. Thanks very much.'

'Excellent. See you then,' said Tomas.

***

The following Friday, Josh woke up feeling really nervous about meeting Tomas. So far, he'd only ever really spoken about his work woes to his friends and wasn't sure what to expect from his time with Tomas. The morning seemed to go by pretty quickly. At 12.20, he made his way out of the office and began walking in the direction of Mr Woodes's office.

When he got to the building, he signed in at reception and made his way up to the offices of TW Capital on the top floor.

Sheree was waiting outside the lift when it opened. She smiled, greeted Josh, and took him to Mr Woodes's office. He was on the phone when they entered. Tomas smiled and gestured for Josh to take a seat.

It was a very large and spacious office with a great view of the city's landscape, including the spire of St. Paul's Cathedral. Josh looked around and noticed an array of pictures all over one side of the wall. They looked like family, friends, and possibly clients as well. On the other side of the room was a very large bookshelf, completely full.

He must be quite the reader, Josh thought.

Two minutes later, Tomas finished his call and got up from his desk.

He was much taller and looked a lot fitter than Josh had expected. Not quite the grey, old, wise man he had imagined him to be.

'Really great to meet you, Josh,' Tomas said, offering a very warm handshake.

'Thanks for making the time to see me.'

'Well, Paul was quite insistent and hinted that the situation was somewhat critical. He also said something about not wanting to have a depressed best man.'

Josh offered a nervous laugh. *Note to self,* he thought. *Kick Paul in the shins for making me out to be desperate.*

Sheree came back with some coffee for Josh and water for Tomas.

Josh had noticed a few trophies on the bookshelf, including a recent squash trophy. He and Paul had become close friends while playing on the squash team at university. He wondered how on earth Tomas found the time to play considering he clearly had a very busy schedule. He asked him about it.

'I get to play at least once a fortnight with one of my associates or clients, so I guess you could say I mix business with pleasure. I also make it a point to get to the gym at least three times a week. I enjoy keeping fit and healthy, but I also find that it actually helps keep me mentally alert as I go about my business.'

They talked about squash and sports for a while before Tomas said, 'So, tell me about your situation.'

Josh wasn't sure where to begin. In the end, he started by telling him of the aspiration he had had as a little boy to become a doctor.

'I remember writing a letter to my first primary school teacher. She was an excellent teacher,' said Josh. 'Anyway, it was shortly after moving schools. I wrote about wanting to become one of the best doctors in the world. I must've been about nine or ten at the time. I even got a part-time job in a hospital when I was seventeen just so that I could get some relevant experience, but when the time came, I was turned down by every medical school I applied to despite having a number of interviews at some of the best universities, including Oxford.'

'Do you know why that was?' asked Tomas.

'Do you mean why it was that I was turned down?' replied Josh, taking a sip of his coffee.

Tomas nodded.

'I'm not really sure. Lots of competition, I guess. Apparently, one of the universities felt that I wasn't really cut out for medicine or particularly interested in science.'

'I see. That must've been really disappointing.'

'It was devastating, actually,' said Josh. It was still quite a painful memory. 'Anyway, I ended up studying for a degree in physics and management.'

'That's not easy either, though you probably had less studying to do. How did you find that?'

'Strangely enough, the best parts for me were the management units and giving presentations on group or individual coursework. I didn't really enjoy the physics units.'

'So, why did you choose physics and not something else?' asked Tomas.

'I don't know. I felt completely lost after I didn't get into medical school and didn't really know what to do. I thought about psychology for a while, and then I bounced ideas around with a few people, including an uncle who had done a management degree and had worked with lots of people. So, I guess I figured that was probably worth doing. I think I picked physics just to keep the science connection. Anyway, I graduated six years ago with an Upper Second, but I still feel a bit lost about the direction I should go in and what I really want do. I like working with people—that much I know. But I've just found most of my jobs pretty unfulfilling.'

'So what exactly made you want to become a doctor?'

'Er … Well, my dad died of cancer when I was about six. I don't remember much about his death; however, as I grew up, I realised that doctors improve people's lives. I guess I wanted to make a difference in people's lives.'

'That's always a noble reason,' Tomas said sincerely. 'And what are you doing now?'

'Well, for the last six months, almost, I've been working for Inspired Marketing as a marketing assistant. Most of our clients refer to us as IM. We work on a lot of national campaigns, which you would think are pretty exciting, but most of my work is the boring market research and literature distribution stuff. I've only been to two client meetings. When I got the job, I thought every day would be different. I thought that one day I'd be developing a marketing campaign schedule and the next day drafting press releases or dealing with clients. Maybe even travelling to exhibitions or something like that. But so far, it's been mostly boring work, and my manager—'

Tomas politely jumped in. 'I know IM very well. We're one of your clients, and your CEO, Mick, has been my squash partner on several occasions.'

Tomas noticed the surprised look on Josh's face and reassured him.

'My conversations with Mick are usually about business and not staffing matters. Anyway, to me, it sounds like you're being given a good grounding in the basics before being thrown in the deep end, which always pays off in the long run. After all, if you master the basics, you're more likely to be entrusted with greater responsibilities, don't you think?'

'I don't know about that,' said Josh dismissively. He hesitated, leaned forward in his chair, and then said, 'Can I be honest?'

'Of course.'

'I just think my manager is too demanding. He's always complaining about my attitude, about how slow I work, and yet he can't even give me exciting tasks to do.'

'Hmmm … You said you've only been with IM for about six months. Where were you before that?'

Josh grimaced as he pondered the question. 'Well, my first two jobs were with a pharmaceutical company. I joined their two-year graduate training scheme and ended up in the medical technology department afterwards, but I found that pretty boring. I didn't enjoy the design and development work, even though I was working with cutting-edge technology. I also wanted to try something new and thought I'd find what I was really passionate about outside the company. So, after being with the company for four years, I handed in my resignation.'

'You mean you left without securing something first?'

'Er … Yes,' said Josh, looking away.

'That was a brave move.'

'Well, it didn't turn out as I'd hoped. I tried to join one of the big consulting firms, but nothing transpired. I found it difficult finding work for several months. Eventually, I took on some temporary jobs for about a year before I got this job with IM. So far, it just feels like nothing has been the right fit for me.'

'You know, thirty years ago, most people would've been happy with just about any job and stuck with that. Nowadays, young people, especially, seem to have higher expectations and are often quicker to move if they feel their skills are not being used to the full.'

Josh simply nodded in agreement.

Tomas took a sip of water, looked at the clock on the wall, and continued. 'I don't actually think that's a bad thing entirely. However, in my experience, whether you stay in one organisation or not, the people who do really well in their careers are the ones who don't see themselves as victims of their circumstances.'

'What do you mean?' said Josh as he shifted uncomfortably in his seat.

'Well, I may be wrong, but it sounds like you think job satisfaction and having a great career begins with what is happening around you, all the external things that you may or may not be able to control, rather than your attitude and what is happening within.'

'I certainly don't feel like I've been lucky with any of my choices or jobs so far,' said Josh rather defensively.

Tomas was silent for a while and then said, 'I'll never forget something my dad told me when I was growing up. He said, "Don't ever let yourself become a passenger in your own life. Always stay in the driver's seat." That was his way of saying I should always be proactive and take responsibility for where I'm at in life and where I want to get to. That was great advice.'

'Hmmm …' Josh felt that was more like a subtle telling off than great advice.

Tomas drank some of his water and then said, 'The reason that I'm going to France this afternoon is because I'll be speaking to a group of MBA students on Monday at the INSEAD graduate business school in Fontainebleau, near Paris. I'm giving one of my regular lectures on The Next Generation of Leadership. One of the things I always stress is the importance of being inquisitive, reading biographies, and learning from the experiences of others. I think it's extremely valuable as we navigate paths that others have already been down.'

Josh glanced over at the bookshelf. 'I noticed you had a lot of books over there,' he said.

'Half of those are biographies or autobiographies,' said Tomas.

'To be honest, apart from the documents and articles I have to read and research for work, I'm not much of a reader. I've done my fair share of studying at uni. Besides, right now, I can barely find the time to work through my own thoughts and ideas, not to mention taking on someone else's.'

'Well, you've got to ask yourself how helpful your own ideas have been to date,' said Tomas.

Ouch!

'Books are great,' continued Tomas, 'because they have the ability to expand your thinking, even if you don't agree with everything in them, and you can also access the ideas in your own time whenever you want to.'

'Yeah, that's true,' said Josh half-heartedly.

'Of course, as I mentioned, another great way of expanding your thinking and perspective is by speaking to experienced people around you,' said Tomas.

'I guess so, but I don't think I'd know where to start or what exactly I'd really want to learn from them,' said Josh.

'Well, you could ask questions about their careers or businesses. I'm sure you'll gain some interesting insights from that alone.'

'Yeah, but would people like that really be willing to make time for me? They're usually so busy.'

'Oh, I think most experienced people would gladly share their pearls of wisdom with anyone who shows a genuine hunger to learn. Granted, they're often very busy, but you don't know if you don't ask.'

'Well, it's worth a try at least,' said Josh, somewhat convinced.

'Isn't IM involved in the European Business Leaders Convention next month?' asked Tomas.

'Yes, that's right. We're organising the marketing campaigns.'

'Are you planning to attend then?'

'It hadn't crossed my mind. I'm carrying out research for a few other campaigns, so probably not. Besides, I wouldn't want to take on any more work right now. I'm already behind on a few deadlines as it is.'

Glancing at the clock, Tomas said, 'I need to leave for the airport shortly. Listen, if I were you, I'd find a way to help out with the convention and use that as an opportunity to speak to some of the business people there. I'm presenting an award on the night, so I'll also be there.'

'It might be a challenge, but I'll see what I can do.'

'You have nothing to lose,' offered Tomas.

They both smiled and stood up from their chairs.

Sheree's desk was right outside Tomas's office, so Tomas walked outside with Josh and spoke with her briefly. He then said goodbye to Josh and excused himself to make a few phone calls before setting off for the airport.

That wasn't so bad, Josh thought as he made his way back to his office.

∗∗∗

That evening, Josh had a long chat with Paul about his meeting with Tomas and his suggestion about the convention.

'Sounds like it's time for you to get back into the driver's seat,' said Paul with a smile.

'Yeah, let's just hope I don't get pulled over for reckless driving,' replied Josh.

They both laughed.

'What do you think of the convention idea?' asked Josh.

'Hey, I'd definitely go for it if I were you.'

'I don't think my manager's going to be too keen to swap my project.'

'Can't you offer to make up the time?' asked Paul.

'Yeah. Maybe. I'll see. He doesn't like me as it is.'

'Give it a try.'

The following day, Josh spoke to Lewis about the convention. Lewis wasn't eager for him to get involved, but he was eventually persuaded by Josh's insistence that he would keep on top of the other deadlines.

'I guess we could do with an extra hand on the night,' Lewis finally relented.

Summary of Principles and Lessons

Getting a good grounding in the basics before being thrown into the deep end always pays off in the long run.

Master the basics in my job. That way, I am more likely to be entrusted with greater responsibility.

The people who do really well in their careers don't see themselves as victims of their circumstances.

I should always be proactive and take responsibility for where I'm at in life and where I want to go.

Whatever my situation, there is always something I can do about it if I am proactive and take responsibility.

Be inquisitive, read biographies, and learn from the experience of others.

2—Commit to Excellence Now

The price of success is hard work, dedication to the job at hand, and the determination that whether we win or lose, we have applied the best of ourselves to the task at hand.

—Vince Lombardi

In the weeks leading up to the convention, Josh did some research to find out who would be attending. It was an impressive mix of business people—more than three hundred CEOs, entrepreneurs, non-executive directors, and senior executives from a variety of backgrounds, and they represented more than thirty industries and eighty organisations. About thirty percent of the attendees were female from what he could tell.

On the day of the convention, Josh's task, along with Kelly, who was Pete's executive assistant, and five other junior creatives, was to man the registration desk. When the guests started arriving, he was on the lookout for Tomas.

He noticed him about fifteen minutes before the event was due to kick off.

'Hi, Josh. I see you made it,' said Tomas as he picked up his nametag from the desk.

'Yeah. Well, I thought I'd take your advice and come along.'

'Are you coming in shortly?' asked Tomas.

'I think so. I'm not sure how long I'll be needed out here.'

'Well, come and look for me at the end. I'd be happy to introduce you to a few people.'

'Great. Thanks!'

About thirty minutes after the programme commenced, Lewis came over to speak with Josh, Kelly, and the others. Josh had barely seen him all evening.

'Thanks for your help, guys,' said Lewis. 'You're welcome to stay till the end and enjoy some refreshments or leave if you have something to do. Todd and I will clear up the registration table afterwards and take all of this stuff back to the office.'

Kelly said she had a few things to do and so would leave early. Josh offered to stay till the end, as did two of the creatives.

At the end of the main programme, during the networking session, Josh went to find Tomas. He saw him close to the front of the room where he was laughing with two executives. He suddenly felt a bit out of place and considered making an early getaway.

Just as he began to turn away, a voice called out, 'Hey, Josh!' He looked up. It was Tomas.

He walked over to where they were standing. Holding Josh's shoulder, Tomas introduced him to the two executives as a young professional on a quest. One of them, Martin, was the head of an international engineering company. The other executive, Sonya, was the senior partner in a city law firm.

'Sounds like you're in the right place,' said Martin. 'I'm the CEO of a global engineering company, and I still don't know what I want to be when I grow up.'

They all laughed.

Maybe they're human after all, thought Josh.

He told them a bit about his situation.

As they began to talk and describe their careers to Josh, Tomas excused himself. 'You're in good hands,' he said to Josh.

'I think it's worth figuring out exactly why you're not enjoying your job, but whatever you do,' said Sonya, 'don't use that as an excuse to slack off. You've got to remain positive and committed to giving your best in the moment. After all, even the best jobs in the world aren't perfect. Personally, though I've enjoyed most of my jobs, this is the first job where I've actually loved more than ninety percent of it. It's not always that way, especially in the early stages of your career.'

'Does that mean I should do something that I don't enjoy?'

'Not at all,' answered Martin. 'But I've observed that a lot of young professionals often have expectations that create a mismatch. You've got to ask yourself how much effort you're putting in and how hard you're working to make the job work for you. It's also worth considering whether you have a set of expectations about your employer that are unrealistic, like giving you a high level of responsibility before you've even mastered the basics.'

'I hear what you're saying. I just think that most of my employers haven't been great at giving me the type of tasks or variety I need in order to get really excited about my work.'

Sonya smiled and said, 'Remember that old cliché: Rome wasn't built in a day. We've all been there. There's life experience that goes with success. Young professionals aren't immediately trusted to take on significant responsibility in an organisation because they need time to develop judgement and know what skills to apply when. I remember feeling like a slave in my first job, always being told what to do. However, I was given the opportunity to work alongside some truly outstanding people and saw that as a great experience—one that I wouldn't change in a million years.'

'That's interesting,' said Josh.

Martin spoke. 'You know, it took me a while to realise that the world of work is here to meet the needs of the organisation at large and not simply my individual needs. Of course, it's absolutely in the interest of any organisation to develop you. Right now, one of my main priorities is increasing the leadership and management capabilities in my organisation. I definitely see staff development as critical to the success and growth of any organisation. Having said all that, I've observed time and time again that those who go on to do really well in their careers are the ones who take full responsibility for their growth and development and avoid playing the blame game.'

'Sounds like something Tomas said when I first met him.'

'Well, he and Martin are right,' said Sonya. 'Job satisfaction is less about what the employer gives you and more about what you make of the job. I don't go to work primarily hoping that someone would satisfy my job needs. I go there as a producer of value. These days, I think there's a lot of autonomy even in the most mundane of jobs, so you can be creative in how you add value and expand your satisfaction. Before I went into corporate law, I started out working for a law firm where I was mostly involved in supporting criminal cases. It wasn't always pleasant. I only got a lot of job satisfaction by being creative and committed to learning from those around me. While you're figuring things out, my advice would be to find ways to enrich your experience at work.'

'Are you saying it would be wrong for me to leave a job if I thought it wasn't the right fit?'

'Well, that could just be a knee-jerk reaction because you think the grass is greener elsewhere,' replied Sonya. 'The way I look at it is that, as your career develops, you really want each move to represent progress, which shows that you're becoming more valuable and competent at what you do. On the other hand, there's an old Turkish proverb I often tell my children: No matter how far you go down the wrong road, turn back! It's better to move on than to commit to something your heart isn't into. Just be wary that potential employers may think you lack judgement and staying power when they see so much movement on your CV. Sometimes, you've got to do things that you're not particularly excited about. It's all part of the learning process.'

'I'm sure you're right,' replied Josh. 'I honestly expected the answers to be simpler than this. I wish it were a bit more black and white.'

Martin looked at his watch and then said, 'I have to leave in a few minutes, but as Sonya mentioned earlier, it's definitely worth considering why you don't enjoy your job. Otherwise, there's a danger that you'll react emotionally to something that might just be a temporary situation and find yourself jumping ship for the wrong reasons. It needs to be a considered decision. Ultimately, if you can find no good resolve, move decisively. Just remember that in many cases, what you think is a terrible situation turns out to be pretty beneficial to your career. It's what you make of the opportunity that is really important. Early on in my career, even though I wasn't clear about what I wanted to achieve in the long-term, I committed to doing an excellent job within my area of responsibility. It made all the difference.'

'So I should just persevere then?'

'Perseverance is certainly an essential quality of people who end up doing anything really well. I think it's important to have a healthy level of patience and willingness to let something grow on you and not give up too quickly.'

'I guess so. You've certainly given me a lot of food for thought,' said Josh.

He thanked them for their time and then remembered a tip Paul had given him. He asked if he could keep in touch with them.

Martin gave Josh his business card and said he was happy for Josh to do so.

'I'll be travelling quite a bit over the next few months, so it might be difficult to get hold of me even via email,' Martin said.

Sonya said she was also happy for Josh to keep in touch. 'I may not reply quickly, but I always get 'round to it at some point.'

He thanked them again and excused himself to chat with a few other people.

Ten minutes later, he was engrossed in a conversation with Tomas, CJ, who was a retail entrepreneur, and Paula, a non-executive director of a large insurance firm.

By the end of the night, he had made a few notes to review later. His head was reeling from all the advice. He asked Tomas if it would be okay to chat through some of the ideas with him. Tomas agreed and suggested he get in touch with Sheree to schedule a catch-up in a few weeks' time. Josh said his goodbyes.

The next day, Josh got up very early; he was so intrigued by the various conversations he'd had at the convention that he wanted to review some of the key points.

As he read through, he compared them to some of the scribbles from his first meeting with Tomas.

This all makes sense, but it still doesn't change the fact that I'm doing something I don't enjoy.

Summary of Principles and Lessons

Commit to remaining positive and doing my current job well

Take responsibility for my career direction

Find ways to enrich my work experience—my job is what I make of it

Remember that there's life experience that goes with success

Be realistic about the responsibilities I expect my employer to give to me

Be strategic—don't make decisions with long-term impact for short-term reasons such as leaving a job just because it isn't satisfying

Sometimes, what I think is a terrible situation can turn out to be pretty beneficial for my career—it's all about what I make of it

Perseverance is an essential quality of people who end up doing anything really well

It's important to have a healthy level of patience and willingness to let something grow on me and not give up too quickly

3—Prepare for the Waves

Life is a series of experiences, each one of which makes us bigger, even though sometimes it is hard to realise this. For the world was built to develop character, and we must learn that the setbacks and grief which we endure help us in our marching onward.

—Henry Ford

'Has someone died? Why that look on your face?' asked Paul.

It was 6.30 in the morning and both Paul and Josh were about to leave for work.

'What can I say? It's my favourite day of the week! We'll have the usual Monday morning briefing and then I have the sweet privilege of spending most of the time doing ridiculous paperwork, research, and making calls.'

'Someone's in a foul mood.'

'You think?'

Paul put his jacket on and began looking for his car keys on the coffee table in the middle of the room.

Josh sat down. 'Maybe what's really getting to me is that I've come to the end of my six-month probation and I've got a meeting with Lewis and Pete this afternoon to discuss my performance.'

'So what's the problem?' asked Paul, still looking for his keys.

'Well, I'm not exactly expecting to receive the employee of the month award.'

'It can't be that bad.'

Josh just shrugged. 'Are you looking for those?' he asked while pointing to a set of keys on the unit underneath the TV.

'Ah, there they are. Thanks. By the way, how come Pete's involved?'

'I think it's because he set my original performance targets before Lewis joined IM. Maybe I'm feeling more nervous because he'll be there.'

'I can see why. Listen, I'm sure it'll go well. I've got to dash, but I've got my fingers crossed for you,' he said as he headed for the front door.

Josh offered half a smile.

'I'll need it,' he said to himself quietly as he picked up his bag and got ready to head out the door.

***

At 3 p.m., Josh, Lewis, and Pete gathered in Pete's office.

Most of the staff at IM were avid football fans. Pete was no exception. He talked about some of the weekend football matches before turning to the document in front of him. Lewis had sent a summary of Josh's performance to Josh and Pete at the end of the previous week to review before the meeting. Josh hadn't looked at the summary.

Without looking up, Pete asked Josh how he thought his work was going.

'I think it's going well,' Josh answered, avoiding eye contact with Lewis.

They spent the next forty-five minutes discussing each one of his six performance targets.

'As it stands, you're only on target to meet half of these,' summarised Lewis. 'If you start paying more attention to the quality of your work and meeting deadlines, then I'm sure we'll notice significant improvements.'

'I really believe you've got what it takes,' said Pete. 'I just don't see the same hunger you had when you first joined IM.'

'Well …' Josh hesitated. 'You're right. I'll do my best.' He didn't want to discuss how he was really feeling in case Pete didn't understand. He certainly didn't want to speak about it in front of Lewis.

Pete said Josh had two months to turn things around.

Josh thanked Pete and Lewis and then slowly walked out of the office.

How can I turn things around when I can barely find the motivation to get through Monday morning?

***

'So what did you think?'

This was Josh's first meeting with Tomas since the convention three weeks ago. Josh had called and left a thank-you message with Sheree the following day. He'd also sent thank-you emails to Sonya, Martin, CJ, and Paula. All of whom replied, except Martin.

'Well, at first I felt a little bit intimidated by all the people in the room. They all seemed so sure of themselves. But it didn't take me long to realise they were normal. They certainly had a lot of great advice to offer. My head was spinning by the end of the evening, but I jotted down some of the main ideas I picked up.'

He pulled out his iPad, found his notes, and slid it across the table to Tomas.

Tomas smiled as he read Josh's notes. 'It looks like you picked up quite a bit from your conversations. Well done.'

'Thanks.'

Josh grinned as he looked at his notes. *Yeah, I did remember quite a bit,* he thought.

Tomas continued. 'Of course, the real value comes when you make this part of your character and not just a collection of useful ideas. That way, when the waves of life come hitting hard, you have the resilience to stand your ground.'

Josh's grin turned into a slight frown.

'I guess so. I must admit that, although this all makes sense, I'm still not enjoying what I'm doing.'

'You'd be surprised how few people start off with their ideal role or with their lives all mapped out. For most people, it's a journey where things unfold as you go along. The hardest part is enjoying the journey.'

'Yeah, well, it's probably too late now anyway.'

'Why do say that?'

'I had my performance review meeting last week, and it wasn't pleasant. I've got two months to turn things around.'

Pointing to Josh's summary, Tomas said, 'You've got a great starting point there. I'm sure you can turn things around, if you're prepared to shine at whatever you're doing and commit to excellence.'

'That's really difficult to do when you're bored.'

'Doing the boring jobs really well and making them interesting is a decision, nothing else.'

'Yes, but a painful one. The thing is I just don't feel motivated by most of my work. I like working closely with our clients when I get the chance, but that's such a small part of what I do, which means most of my time is spent doing work I just don't enjoy. And even though my probation has been extended by a few months, it's not as though I have that much control over what activities I will or won't do.'

'I'm sure that isn't true,' said Tomas.

'Maybe not, but it really is a challenge keeping myself motivated to even do my work, not to mention do it well.'

'For most people, simply putting food on the table is motivation to stick at something and keep working,' said Tomas.

'That's what makes it worse. Sometimes I think I should just be grateful for what I have and what I'm doing, but I can't seem to shake the restlessness I feel. How do you do it? How do you keep yourself motivated on a daily basis?'

'That's a great question. For me, it starts with keeping in mind the overall vision of what I'm trying to achieve in business and in my life in general. And then I write down the three most important things for the day that will make it a successful day in light of my purpose. That keeps me motivated, especially because I know I'm concentrating on activities that are helping me achieve a bigger purpose linked to my company's vision and my personal vision. It could be a meeting with a client, reviewing a new investment strategy, carrying out a performance review with one of my senior associates, or discussing a new community project.'

'I'm usually just told what to do. That's my company vision.'

'Are you saying you don't know what IM's overall vision and goals are?'

'Er ... Yes. Sort of.'

'If you're not really sure, then I recommend you spend some time getting a good understanding of what they are. I'm sure you could speak to your manager or even look on

IM's website. Whatever you do, it's so important that you see and keep in mind the link between what you're doing at work each day and the overall vision and goals.'

'I guess I should be a bit embarrassed that I'm not sure. Something is always said about our company vision and goals at our monthly staff meetings, but I usually switch off because I've never really considered how it applies to me directly since I'm not a manager.'

Josh made a few notes on his iPad.

He looked up at Tomas. 'What about my personal vision? That's probably what I'm more interested in.'

'That requires a lot more effort on your part and means taking the time to answer a series of important questions about what you really want for yourself personally and professionally.'

Tomas reached over and picked up a large, brown, leather folder on his table and pulled out a piece of paper. 'Here's something I've used for myself over the years and keep revisiting.'

It was a list of handwritten questions.

Josh skimmed over them and frowned. 'This looks like a lot of work. Is it really necessary?' he asked.

'Remember a great career takes thought and effort; it doesn't just happen,' said Tomas.

'I know, I know. I just feel that things need to turn around quickly or I won't even have a job. Like you said, that should be motivation enough, just trying to keep my job.'

He folded the piece of paper and put it in his coat pocket. 'I've made a note about reviewing IM's corporate goals and possibly speaking to my manager. I think I'll start there for now.'

'OK. There is one other thing that keeps me motivated, and that's keeping fit and active. Come to think of it, didn't you mention that you play squash?'

'Uh … Yes, but I haven't played in a while.'

'Rory, my finance director, has just signed us up to be part of a business squash league with Riverview Leisure Club.'

'I think I've heard of them. Ah, yes. Paul and Jaz thought about using it for their wedding reception, but they've gone for a Marriott hotel instead because Jaz gets a good deal. I thought it was called The Riverside Centre?'

'It was, but they changed ownership about two months ago. Anyway, they've got excellent sporting facilities, including several squash courts. TRC used to run an individual squash league, which I've been part of for the last three years. RLC have now changed things around slightly and introduced a business league, which they plan to run once a year for twenty-six weeks. It's open to companies or groups of players to enter a team of six. The good thing about this league is that team members can play for each other, so if I'm out of town on business, or anyone else for that matter, we don't lose points because someone in the team can cover our game without us having to forfeit or reschedule.'

'That sounds good. I don't think IM will be signing up a team though. Most of the staff are football crazy and that's it.'

'Actually, I was thinking about you joining us,' said Tomas.

'Oh. Er … I didn't see that coming.'

'We're a team member short and it would be useful to have someone to complete the team who isn't exactly new to the game. Do you remember CJ from the convention?'

'The retail entrepreneur?'

'Yes. He's also putting a team together. He's a member of the RLC and another one of my regular squash partners. We've also played against each other in a few competitions. You might find it a very worthwhile networking opportunity considering that RLC has quite an exclusive membership.'

'Well, when you put it like that, I guess I couldn't possibly say no. I have actually been thinking about doing something just to keep fit, and I'm hopeless at football, so this is probably as good a time as any.'

'Great! Looks like we've got our team. I'll let Rory know and ask Sheree to send you all the details. It's a Monday league and starts a week on Monday.'

Josh thanked Tomas and made his way back to the office.

Summary of Principles and Lessons

I develop character by putting into practice good advice. That way, when the waves of life come hitting hard, I have the resilience to stand my ground.

Very few people start with their ideal role or with their lives all mapped out. For most people, it's a journey where things unfold as they go along.

Overcoming boredom is a matter of making a decision to do the boring jobs really well.

To maintain my motivation, I should keep in mind the big picture of what I'm trying to achieve in my work, and then at the beginning of each day, I should write down the three most important things to make it a successful day.

A great career takes planning; it doesn't just happen.

4—Cultivate the Right Habits

Thoughts lead on to purposes; purposes go forth in action; actions form habits; habits decide character; and character fixes our destiny.

—Tryon Edwards

On the first day of the business league, Josh met up with Tomas, Rory, and the three other TWC Associates at Riverview Leisure Club at 6.30 in the evening.

After introductions, Rory said, 'There'll be a briefing session for all the teams in about thirty minutes. From what I've gathered so far, the first two weeks of the league are scheduled as friendly matches only. Weeks twenty-three and twenty-four are scheduled as doubles matches only and will be played in RLC's new doubles court. Only one pair is needed from each team for the doubles matches. The only snag is that the pair has to stay the same for both weeks, so I suggest we decide the pairing nearer the time.'

Josh was relieved that the tournament wasn't going to kick off immediately. He wanted a bit of time to find his game again.

After the briefing session by the RLC representative, they all went to the changing rooms and then proceeded to the courts.

The night went well for team TWC. Overall, they played twelve short matches and won eight. As they were only friendly matches, it was the best of three games and not five. The scores didn't count this week, but both Tomas and Rory thought it was a positive sign for the team.

Josh narrowly lost both of his matches. He expressed disappointment but was secretly pleased with himself. *I don't think I did too badly, considering I haven't played for a few years,* he thought.

As it was the opening night of the business squash league, RLC hosted a reception in its new Riverview Restaurant for all the players. Everyone stayed casually dressed.

Tomas and Rory knew quite a few people there. Tomas pointed out a group to Josh. It was CJ, Sonya, and one person he didn't know.

Josh went over to say hi. Sonya explained that she was a member of the club and had just finished using the gym. She didn't play squash but a team from her law firm was in the league.

'When Tomas told me TWC had entered a team, I thought this might be an opportunity to get my own back,' said CJ.

Josh looked confused.

'He lost to Tomas in the finals last year as part of TRC's singles squash league,' explained Sonya.

'I see,' said Josh. 'So TWC is the team to beat?'

'I don't know about that,' CJ replied quickly. 'Tomas is definitely an exceptional player, but this is a team league; I'd say it depends on how good the rest of the team are. Also, I can imagine that with his schedule he won't be able to play every game he's put down for. Neither will I for that matter, but I've got a really good team.'

'I'm sure we'll put up a good fight,' said Josh.

'If I know Tomas, it'll be more than a good fight!' said Sonya.

They all laughed.

The other person with them was Adam, who Sonya mentioned was a senior vice president of a large software company. Josh thought he looked far too young to be a senior vice president. They discussed the tournament schedule for a while before Josh politely changed the subject and asked their advice on how to stay motivated at work.

'I'm sure it's different for each person,' began Adam. 'Personally, I spend a lot of my time focusing on activities that are both interesting to me and of value to my company. Even if you're not in the position that I'm in where you have lots of control over your work, I think you can still identify activities that are interesting and find a way of making it valuable to the organisation.'

'But isn't it important to feel like you're doing something that's always personally enjoyable as well as worth doing?'

'In an ideal world, I'm sure most people would choose a job that's always enjoyable,' replied Adam. 'However, it often helps me to think of life as a play or a movie. You can't always write the script and there are times when you don't want the part you're given, but you can still mould it into something that fits you. I think you can still keep yourself motivated until your part changes.'

'I agree,' said CJ. 'Before starting my retail businesses, I had several very challenging but boring jobs. I would often give myself treats as a way of increasing my motivation. Of course, I had to be careful not to overdo it.'

'Oh, I remember doing that as well,' said Sonya. 'Although, as I look back, I don't think I've ever worked in an organisation where I haven't believed that what we're doing is important. I think that has also helped.'

'That's lucky,' said Josh.

'I wouldn't put it down to luck. For me, it was about making good decisions and being clear about what I did and didn't enjoy, and then instead of complaining I took action to change what I could.'

'I couldn't agree more,' said CJ. 'The high flyers across my businesses have stood out to me not because they've always had the most interesting work or best ideas but because they've shown the right attitude towards their work, developed the right habits, and given it their all. I've got numerous anecdotes about young professionals on our fast-track management programme who would manage their diary to include motivating activities, especially when the projects they were working on were a bit mundane. I can predict that they're the ones who will very quickly move into a position where they have more control over the type of work they get and do.'

Josh mulled over CJ's last statement.

They shared a few more stories before Josh thanked them for their time. He said his goodbyes to Tomas and the others before making an exit.

'Well done, tonight,' said Rory, patting Josh on the shoulder.

As he made his way home, Josh kept returning to CJ's comment about the young professionals in his businesses moving into a position where they had more control over their work.

Maybe I need to move up the chain at work. Then I'd probably have the freedom to do the jobs I like the most and delegate the rest.

***

Three days later, as they sipped their drinks in the patisserie near Tomas's office, Josh showed Tomas his notes from the other night.

'It looks like you're laying a good foundation.'

'I hope so. By the way, I've been thinking about something CJ said. He talked about some of the young professionals across his businesses moving into a position where they had more control over their work. I figured that if I can get some sort of team leader role at IM, I'll probably be able to do what I want and delegate the rest.'

'There's more to team leading than delegating what you don't want to do.'

'I'm sure there is, but I bet it'll give me more control than I have now. Oh, and there was something else CJ talked about the other night that I overlooked at the time, but on reflection I wasn't really sure what he meant. It was something about the high achievers in his company developing the right habits. What exactly are the right habits?'

'He was probably talking about habits that help you succeed in your career.'

'Like what?' quizzed Josh.

'I'm sure you'll get different views depending on who you ask, but I can give you my top four.'

'OK.'

'Number one for me is building and maintaining strong relationships. Whether you're working in an organisation for someone else or running your own organisation like CJ or me, you don't get to the top, or even excel for that matter, just because you're great. If you can't take people with you, eventually you're going nowhere.'

'So you're saying you've got to be good with people?'

'Not just *good* with people—*great* with people! All the people I know who have had genuine success value people and believe passionately in the power of networks. They also understand how to connect with and influence people at different levels, which comes from understanding what matters to them and knowing how to tailor your interactions.'

'Some people might say that's being a bit manipulative,' Josh said. 'Why can't it just be about how good you are and not about who you know?'

'Ultimately, business and life are about relationships, so there's no question that it's crucial to build and maintain great relationships and networks, but yes, you've still got to be known as someone who does a great job. It's not mutually exclusive.'

'I see,' said Josh adding some notes to his iPad.

'The next thing is developing a strong passion, drive, or sense of purpose. I know and see a lot of people who dread getting up and going to work on a Monday morning. They have so little enthusiasm or excitement for what they do because they've got no clear passion or purpose. They fail to see the incredible opportunity work provides to grow in character and unleash our potential for greatness.'

'I've never thought of work that way. That's quite a description!'

'Well, when you have a clear sense of purpose and passion, it puts the highs and the lows of each day into perspective.'

'I guess so. And the third?'

'For me, the third habit is being productive—not just active.'

Josh looked puzzled. 'What's the difference?'

'I always say to my staff that our aim isn't to invest in new ventures or make acquisitions just for the sake of it. Instead, our aim is to ensure we're investing in the right places, at the right time, and for the right reasons. That's being productive. It takes thought and determination and is much harder than you think. Not only does it mean we've got to be clear about our overall goals, it also means that we constantly have to challenge ourselves and ask ourselves if what we're doing at any given time is adding value and focused on the overall vision or whether it's simply killing time.'

'Ah, that makes sense. Being active is so much easier though.'

'Of course it is. That's why these habits separate the high achievers from the low achievers. That brings me on to one more habit. If you really want to move from the realms of mediocrity, then you need to be hungry for and committed to excellence. That means you've got to set the bar high in whatever you are doing and want to do. I don't believe in being a perfectionist, but if you run through life with low standards, you'll never edge over the bar of mediocrity.'

'That sounds like something my squash coach used to say at uni. Of course that means hard work.'

'Yes, it does. I don't know of any successful person who hasn't worked hard. Even those who seem to have a natural gift or talent for what they do work extremely hard at harnessing and developing that talent. Just look at the world of sports. You don't find athletes simply coasting on their natural talent. Instead, they undergo rigorous training in order to perform at a top level.'

Josh was making notes. 'Yeah, you're right.'

Glancing at his watch, Tomas said, 'Looks like we'll have to continue our conversation another time as I've got to get ready for a board meeting.'

'Sure. Thanks again for today.'

'You're welcome. Remember, knowing this stuff is the easy part. Making it who you are is where the real value is.'

'I'll keep that in mind.'

As Josh made his way to his office building, he was convinced that moving up the ladder at work would solve a lot of his problems, but he felt there was very little chance of that happening if he couldn't even raise his game in his current role. He looked over some of his notes since meeting Tomas, Sonya, and CJ and came up with a plan.

Over the next four weeks, he started making notes during the Monday morning briefings on everything that was being said, whether he thought it applied directly to him or not. He spoke with Pete and Lewis about IM's vision and corporate goals and began referring to them in his research reports to Lewis. He also started writing down the three most important things he felt would make each day successful.

He got some good feedback during an informal performance review meeting with Lewis, which he had initiated. During the meeting, he asked about attending more client meetings since he really enjoyed them. Lewis said that could be arranged. Pete was on an overseas business trip but heard about the informal review and sent an email to Josh saying that he was very impressed with how he was turning things around.

There might just be some hope for me after all, thought Josh after reading Pete's email.

Summary of Principles and Lessons

To keep myself motivated and creative on a daily basis, I can

1) Identify activities that are interesting to me;

2) Take the initiative to mould my role in such a way that fits me;

3) Make good decisions;

4) Be clear about what I do and don't enjoy and take action to change what I can; and

5) Manage my diary to include activities that are motivating.

If I want to be a high achiever, I should

1) Build and maintain strong relationships and networks, effectively connecting with others;

2) Develop a strong passion, drive, or sense of purpose;

3) Stay focused on being productive and not just active; and

4) Have a hunger and commitment to excellence.

Work provides an incredible opportunity to grow in character and unleash my potential for greatness.

5—Embrace the Pain of Growth

When we long for life without difficulties, remind us that oaks grow strong in contrary winds and diamonds are made under pressure.

—Peter Marshall

During week six of the squash league, as he walked into Tomas's office, it suddenly dawned on Josh how much he enjoyed speaking with Tomas. He thought about their first meeting, only a few months earlier, and the sense of anxiety he felt. Now he considered himself rather fortunate that Tomas had agreed to a catch-up every two to four weeks. Josh didn't mind the fact that it usually meant a very early start to fit around his schedule.

After a quick chat about the squash league games and their position on the leader board, Tomas asked Josh how things were going at work.

'Things are certainly much better. I even got a positive informal review from my manager. But if I'm honest, it still feels like I'm living someone else's life. The only difference is that I've finally come to terms with that.'

'From where I stand, I think you're moving in the right direction.'

'Maybe so, but I wish life was easy and everything just fell into place like this,' said Josh, clicking his fingers.

'Yes, that would be nice,' said Tomas with a smile. 'But how else would you build character if life was easy? It's difficult to see it at the time, but you're going through what I call growth pains. If you let the process work properly, it can be quite transformational.'

'I don't see how having a difficult life or challenging job can be transformational,' replied Josh.

'Well, you've probably heard this before, but just think about the caterpillar. In order for it to transform into a butterfly, it's got to struggle out of its cocoon. If you tried to cut short the process by prematurely cutting open the cocoon, it would actually come out with a swollen body, shrivelled wings, and so never fly.'

'That is interesting. I hadn't heard of that.'

'It provides a really great parallel for our lives. The challenges and difficulties we face in life aren't just inevitable, they're essential for building character. If you try to bypass the pain of growth and development in any area, you do so at your peril. Instead of laying a strong foundation, you end up with a weak character and a poor work ethic.'

'I've never thought about it that way before. I'd still say the caterpillar's doing a lot better than me. I'm struggling but not exactly going anywhere. I just feel stuck!'

'I'm sure it was the Dalai Lama who said, "There is freedom within your prison." In other words, it's up to you to look for creative ways to make the most of your situation until there's a change. There's probably more to learn in your current role than you realise. Job satisfaction has a lot to do with your attitude.'

'I'm sure you're right, but even you've talked about the importance of having a sense of purpose and vision. At one stage in my life, I was so clear about what I wanted to become, yet now it's just a shattered dream thanks to those silly medical admission boards. And now I have absolutely nothing to replace it with.'

'Just because your dream had to change doesn't mean your life will be any less significant,' said Tomas.

'But why does it have to change? Not that I'm certain I'd want to be a doctor now anyway. It's just that … Oh, I don't know. Haven't you always had a vision of what you wanted to achieve?'

'Yes and no. I remember when I was eleven years old, I was at a comprehensive school and heard that a girl in the final year had achieved ten grade As in her O levels, and I thought, *I am going to do that.* So yes, I had a short-term vision, but I didn't really have a clear sense of what I wanted to be when I grew up.'

'So you didn't set out to run your own business?'

'Not really. My main goal was simply to do something that I enjoyed and was good at, something that involved leading others because I always enjoyed that type of role, whether it was as a school prefect or sports captain. Anyway, later on I considered studying political science in order to go into politics. Then I thought about law so I could become a judge. I even remember dreaming about becoming an astronaut, especially after hearing and reading about the moon landing.'

'An astronaut? That's a far cry from running a business. So how did you end up running TWC?'

'Well, it's a bit of a long story. My dad had been working for an insurance company for twenty-three years when he died in a car accident at the age of forty-eight.'

'Oh, sorry to hear that.'

'That's OK. Of course, it's a long time ago now. Anyway, you'd think that someone who worked for an insurance company would automatically have adequate life insurance, but, for reasons I'll never know, he chose to opt out of the company's automatic life cover scheme and didn't appear to have any other life cover. So after his death, my mother had to work pretty hard to support all three kids, which meant our lifestyle changed drastically. We had some pretty rough times ahead, especially since I was getting ready to apply for university. My dad had often talked about the importance of being business savvy, so when it came to choosing a degree, I decided to pick a business degree because I felt it would allow me stay flexible and explore different options. I still had my aspiration to do something I enjoyed, something that I was good at and involved leading others. For me, a business degree seemed to fit the bill perfectly.'

'I see. So did you set up TW Capital shortly after your degree?'

'No. Actually, I still wasn't thinking about running my own business when I chose that degree or even after graduation. While I was at university, I secured an internship with a different company every summer and did a variety of part-time and weekend jobs just to pay for my upkeep and …'

'Save for the future?' suggested Josh.

'Maybe, but I really had another motive. You see, working in a variety of industries gave me the opportunity to mix with groups that I wouldn't normally mix with and learn from. So while most of my peers would shoot off home after university or work, I would spend time with the various business owners or managers that I worked for and grill them about their roles and how the business worked. My goal was to understand as much as I could about how businesses operated and the different skills required to make them successful. Most of them knew I was studying for a degree in business, and very soon I was discussing strategies that were being implemented in some of these businesses. Nothing too grand, but it made me realise I had a flair for risk-taking and financial investments. Right after my degree, I was hired by a private equity firm that I had done a summer placement with. They took me on as a business analyst and sponsored both my MA in finance and subsequently my MBA.'

'Wow. I wish I'd been that proactive when I was at uni. How long were you with that company before leaving to set up TWC?'

'I was with them for about ten years and was about to become a partner when we were bought by a foreign company. The owners wanted to retire and decided to cash in on the success of the company. I think that was about four years after finishing my MBA. So here I was, suddenly being presented with a window of opportunity to leave, because under the new ownership I wouldn't be contracted to stay with them for an extra four years, which was part of the deal for the sponsorship of my MBA. I also got a great package from the buyout of management shares.'

'That's amazing. I'd so love to be that lucky.'

Tomas smiled. 'You've probably figured out by now, I don't really believe in luck in the same way that most people do. Seneca, the Roman philosopher, said, "Luck is what happens when preparation meets opportunity." I've come to realise that if you're not prepared and haven't put in the work, when the opportunity comes you won't be *lucky* enough to take advantage of it. I was only thirty-two, but I had put in the work that made it feel like the right time for me to leave, and so I did. I sought out some of the most successful people in the field of investments and private equities and asked them to mentor me as I set up TW Capital. Two of them agreed. The rest, as they say, is history.'

'And smooth sailing, I'm sure.'

'Not by any means. Shortly after I started the business, there was a stock market crash. Lots of potential clients were suddenly playing it safe. The first three years of TWC, we didn't make much profit. At one point, I thought I was going to have to sell my house.'

'Really? That must have been challenging to deal with.'

'It was. Growing up, my dad always went on about viewing setbacks as an opportunity to learn something. It was annoying to hear at the time, but it stuck with me, and learn I did. The other thing that helped me push through was knowing that so many others had succeeded in even more challenging circumstances, so I couldn't help but feel that if they could do it then so could I.'

'Hmmm …'

Josh looked at his watch and suddenly realised he had to leave for an appointment with a new client that IM was in talks with.

'Ooops! I've got to go, but thanks as always for your time.'

'You're welcome. See you on Monday. We've got to move up the leader board. I'm not used to seeing my team outside the top three.'

Behind the warm smile, Josh new Tomas was being very serious.

Josh saluted. 'Yes, sir!'

He got into the lift and thought about the meeting with the new client. Lewis had been so impressed with his performance lately that he asked Josh to join the scoping meeting for this new campaign. This was his first time, and though he felt he should be excited, he actually felt more like a fraud.

'For some strange reason, I still feel like I ought to be doing something else,' he whispered to himself as he made his way out of the building.

Summary of Principles and Lessons

Challenges and difficulties in life are a necessary part of developing and building character.

Even when I feel stuck, I can find creative ways to make the most of my situation until there's a change.

Job satisfaction is more about my attitude than the job itself.

Just because my dream of what I wanted to become had to change, it doesn't mean my life will be any less significant.

If I'm working hard at what I'm doing now, then I'm more likely to be prepared when suitable opportunities come my way.

6—Stay Open and Learn from Every Experience

The person who really thinks learns quite as much from his failures as from his successes.

—John Dewey

It was week ten and Team TWC was still in fourth place on the leader board. RLC also displayed the names of the top ten individuals who had won the most matches. Tomas was in second place. Although he had won all his matches, he'd only played twelve out of sixteen so far. His other matches had been split among the team so didn't count towards his personal score.

Josh had won the least number of matches in the team and was feeling the pressure, even though the rest of the team was quite supportive.

Tomas was out of town, so Rory had played one of his matches and a senior TWC associate, Finn, had played the other.

'As long as we're giving our best each time, that's the main thing,' said Rory at the end of the night, though Josh didn't feel reassured.

Most of the teams went to the restaurant bar afterwards for a few drinks. Josh thought about skipping drinks but then decided to go anyway. After one drink with the team, Josh looked around for CJ or Sonya.

He saw CJ engrossed in a conversation with Adam. He thought it better not to interrupt, but then CJ's eyes caught his and he waved him to come over.

'Hi, CJ. Hi, Adam.'

'How's it going?' said CJ.

'I take it you're not talking about the leader board?' said Josh.

'Oh, I think I can read that pretty well. I bet Tomas isn't too pleased.'

Josh shook his head.

'Seriously though, I was wondering how it's going with your job. Have things improved since our last conversation?'

'They definitely have, but I'd be lying if I said I didn't feel lost. The other day, I was speaking to Tomas about how I had a greater sense of purpose as a child than I do now. That's because I had a clearer vision of what I wanted to become.'

'Children definitely have creative minds, don't they?' asked CJ with a smile. 'But, you know what? They're not as aware of the scale of all the options as we are. I've got so much more vision now than I did when I was a child because I'm aware of so many more possibilities. When you're young, it's harder to plot a course when you've got limited options. It's like trying to use a compass with no pointer or one that only points south.'

'Hmmm … I see what you mean,' said Josh, slowly nodding his head.

'Don't get me wrong. I'm not saying that youngsters are wasting their time if they have a clear idea of what they want to become. What I am saying is that it's important when you're young to stay curious and open. Ask other people what they do. And if you don't know what you want to be when you grow up, that's fine. Anything you do will be good experience. Most people discover more about themselves, the skills they like using, and what they find rewarding to achieve as they actually *do* something.'

'What if you got the wrong job?'

'Who says you have to get the right job immediately?' asked CJ. 'I certainly didn't, but I was open to opportunities and knew that something would come up as long as I kept my ears peeled and paid attention to what was going on.'

'I wish I had heard that when I was growing up.'

Josh turned to Adam who had been quiet all this time. 'What about you, Adam? Did you have a vision of what you wanted to achieve when you were younger?'

'I'd like to say yes, but the honest answer is no. While I was at school, I discovered that I really liked computers and I really liked economics, so I did a computer science and economics degree. I wasn't really sure what I wanted to do with either one. My first job was on the graduate management scheme at one of the largest banks in the world. I did several placements, including one in their trading department, and worked on a project installing new trading software, which went really well. After that, I was convinced I wanted to stay in IT, so I moved into the corporate IT department and was headhunted about seven years later to join this software company.'

Adam continued. 'I think sometimes people narrow themselves off too soon. Whether you're doing GCSEs, A levels, or even a degree, I don't think you can you really map out the next ten or twenty years. Not unless you have a professional calling like medicine. Considering the pace at which the world moves today, it's impossible to predict all that I'm going to do or achieve even in the next five years.'

'Sounds like I need to be patient and let things unfold.'

'You know what they say about patience,' said CJ. 'I think you're doing the right things by speaking to people. Just don't let it get you down in the meantime.'

CJ's phone rang and he excused himself to pick it up. Meanwhile, Josh talked with Adam for a few more minutes before calling it a night.

When he got home, Paul and Tim were watching the news.

'Hey, how's the league going?' asked Tim.

'We're still in fourth place.'

'Not bad. If that were the FA Premiership, you might be on course for the Champions League.'

'How reassuring,' said Josh with half a smile.

After the news, Tim said, 'I'm gonna hit the sack, guys. I've got an early flight to catch tomorrow.'

'Where are you off to this time?' asked Josh.

'I've just started a twelve-week assignment in Rome. It's a joint project between the British and Italian governments, so I'll be in Rome for two weeks and then back here for two weeks, and so on.'

'Great. You'll finally be around to help me plan Paul's bachelor's party.'

'Go easy on me, guys! We've been friends a long time, eh?' said Paul.

Tim and Josh both replied, 'Exactly!'

They all laughed.

As they headed off to sleep, Josh noticed that an email had come from Martin moments earlier.

> Hi, Josh,
>
> Sorry about the delayed response. It was really good to meet you too.
>
> I hope your work situation has improved.
>
> Feel free to keep in touch.
>
> M

Josh looked at the clock. It was almost 11 p.m. He decided to reply nonetheless.

> Hi, Martin,
>
> Thanks for your reply. You're working late. Is that the life of a CEO?

Work situation is much better, but still feeling a bit lost. Not sure what my long-term vision is. Might sound like an odd question, but did you always know you'd be an engineer and then CEO?

Thanks,

Josh

A reply came back about ten minutes later.

I've been doing a lot of travelling over the last eight weeks, visiting some of our international offices. I'm currently in China. Our Shanghai office is opening up a new manufacturing plant on the outskirts of the city. It's nearly seven in the morning. I was just catching up on some emails when I noticed yours from a few weeks ago.

I think I understand your situation. When I was young, I always had a sense of urgency and felt that if I hadn't made it by the time I was twenty-five, then I was a failure. Not that I really knew what I wanted to make it in, but I soon realised that every experience I have is valuable as long as I'm learning from and leveraging those experiences.

When I began working in the engineering industry, it took me a few years to realise what I was really excited about, but then I eventually caught the management bug and started enjoying what I was doing.

So, for me, the vision definitely came much later.

I hope that helps.

M

Josh typed a quick response.

Thanks, Martin. Yes, that is helpful. I used to think I needed to replace or regain my vision immediately or I was in trouble.

I'm beginning to realise that it's OK to explore and let that vision evolve.

After fifteen minutes, Martin still hadn't replied, so Josh headed off to bed.

In the morning, he noticed a response from Martin that had come in shortly after midnight.

And the less pressure you put on yourself, the easier it will be.

Keep in touch.

M

***

Three weeks later, Josh saw an internal vacancy for a new team leader role. He almost ignored it, but then he remembered CJ's comments about having more control over his work. He'd managed to improve his performance considerably over the last few months and thought now was a good time to show initiative.

This could be the very thing that finally proves to Pete and Lewis that I'm motivated to exceed expectations and do a good job.

He applied the very next day.

Summary of Principles and Lessons

Every setback gives me an opportunity to learn something.

Most people discover more about themselves, the skills they like using, and what they find rewarding to achieve as they actually do something.

It's OK to give myself time to let my vision evolve.

Every experience I have is valuable as long as I'm learning from and leveraging those experiences.

7—Take Initiative

People are always blaming their circumstances
for what they are. I don't believe in circumstances.
The people who get on in this world are the people who get
up and look for the circumstances they want, and if they
can't find them, make them.

—George Bernard Shaw

'I can't believe it!'

Josh slumped in the chair on the other side of Tomas's desk and just stared out the window. It was week fifteen of the squash league.

'And to make matters worse, the person they chose instead of me hasn't even been with IM as long as I have.'

'What feedback did you receive afterwards?' asked Tomas.

Josh was silent for a while.

Then he said, 'Well, Pete mentioned that he was very impressed that I went for it; however, he said I needed to gain leadership and team management experience first, which is ridiculous! How can I get the experience if they don't even give me the chance to do the job and then get the experience?'

'That's not uncommon, but there are ways 'round it.'

'Not from where I'm standing. It's a classic catch-22 situation. I can't get the job without the experience and I can't get the experience without the job. How am I supposed to stay motivated and do a great job when they won't even take a chance on me? And I thought I'd been doing so well recently; even Lewis has been impressed. Now it looks like I've just been wasting my time.'

'Do you realise this is actually a great opportunity for you?'

Josh stared blankly at Tomas before saying, 'In what way?'

'Well, first things first. Remember you need to stay motivated and open to learning, whatever the outcome. If you let this demoralise you, you could end up reacting instead of making a proactive move,' said Tomas.

'Well, I already feel like throwing in the towel,' replied Josh.

'I know it's disappointing, but you've got to realise that whenever you go for a new job or promotion, you're asking people to take a risk on you.'

'Even if they know you?' asked Josh.

'Yes, even if they know you. It helps to look at it from an employer's perspective, not your own. For example, there are two ways of pursuing a promotion to a team leader role. You could approach it like most people who, in essence, say, "Give me the job and I'll be the leader." Or you could have this approach: "I'm *already* leading, so you might as well give me the job." Which one do you think is more appealing to managers and employers?'

'I'd say the second one, even though it does come across a bit arrogant.'

'Well, it's about having the right attitude and not projecting arrogance. But you're right. It is the latter. The point is that it's much easier for people to trust you and take a risk on you if you're already undertaking some or most of the tasks and responsibilities required of the next level up. When speaking to my MBA students about job progression, I always insist that if they want to progress to the next level, they need to begin operating at that level long before they're officially there.'

'It sounds a bit obvious when you put it like that. But how do I get the opportunity to do those tasks or take on that responsibility in the first place?'

'I'm sure you can come up with creative ways. When I was working for the private equity firm and aiming for the position of partner, I knew that I needed to gain some experience of managing a business so I shadowed a number of directors within my organisation. Later on, I found people outside the organisation who I admired because they were running successful businesses of their own, and I asked them to mentor me. This was before I even thought about my own business. I even joined the board of trustees for a large charity. All of these extra activities required a huge investment of my time, but the payback was significant in terms of gaining higher level experience in managing businesses, as well as managing and influencing people.'

'I see. So I could find ways to gain the leadership and team management experience by getting involved in activities outside my work?' asked Josh.

'Yes, that's one way,' said Tomas. 'Employers and managers always value individuals who show initiative and who bring relevant, transferable skills that they've picked up elsewhere.'

'Come to think of it, the person who got the job is involved in quite a few projects outside work. I guess she must have gained a lot of additional experience and skills that way,' said Josh.

'It definitely sounds like it. By the way, it's not just about going outside the workplace to gain the experience. There are bound to be many opportunities in your organisation to gain experience and skills above and beyond what you normally would in your main role. If I were in your shoes, I would see this as an opportunity to learn more about myself and gain new skills that will make me more valuable and more competent for that role, or others, for that matter.'

'Wouldn't it be great if this was a standard part of my development journey without having to fight so hard for this myself?' Josh muttered.

Tomas caught on to what he said. 'I think a lot of organisations are committed to creating opportunities for their staff to develop skills and qualities that add value to them and to the organisation. But the fact still remains that it starts with the individual having the right attitude. Remember that developing the skills you need for the next level isn't an excuse to drop the ball in your current role.'

'I know, I know.'

✳✳✳

Later that day, Josh sent an email to Sonya and asked for her advice on dealing with his catch-22. She responded a few days later.

Hi, Josh,

My husband, Chris, works as the people development director for Rupp Warr Linsey, a global advertising firm. He recently told me about two junior account handlers in his organisation who were very keen to move into the creative side of the business—working on advertising ads as junior creatives rather than simply managing client accounts. Instead of moaning about it, they came up with a proposal. They said they would continue to work as junior account handlers but would put in extra time outside normal work hours to gain the experience of creatives. You can imagine that this eventually caught the attention of senior management, including Chris, who gave them the opportunity to move into the creative department, and I hear they are both doing exceptionally well.

What impressed me was that it started with them maintaining the standard of their current performance and coming up with a proposal that didn't compromise that.

I think it's a great example of how to take the initiative to gain experience or skills that you don't have, and it also reinforces the importance of giving your best at what you are doing right now, even if you'd rather be doing something else. That's a sign of character.

If you want my two cents for getting out of a catch-22 as you described it, it's this: have a great attitude, deliver well, maintain a lot of great relationships, and get as much exposure as possible. That also means trying a few things as and when the opportunities come up.

All the best,

S. B.

Josh sent a reply.

Dear Sonya,

Thanks for your response. It's very interesting to hear about the creatives in your husband's company. I should take a leaf out of their book.

I just have to wait till another opportunity comes along.

Thanks,

Josh

The reply from Sonya came a few hours later.

Hi, Josh,

You'll be surprised how many of the best jobs never get advertised.

All the best,

S. B.

Josh made a special note of this.

***

The following Monday, during week sixteen of the squash league, Josh was scheduled to play two matches. His second match was against CJ. He lost the match by three games to one. It was the last match of the evening for both of them.

As they got dressed in the changing room, Josh told CJ about his catch-22.

'I spend some of my time mentoring junior managers within my businesses and come across that a lot,' CJ said. 'I always tell them that when it comes to pursuing a promotion, they've got to be very clear and understand exactly what is required at the next level and how that relates to what they're doing at the moment. That way, they can clearly identify any skill gaps and look for ways to gain the right experiences, either in the workplace or outside. Don't wait to be given a new title before you show initiative. Most bosses that I know have so much to do and so many people making demands of their time, so you'll stand out if you have a different attitude.'

'Sounds like good advice.'

'Have you ever thought about volunteering to take on some of your manager's workload?' asked CJ.

'Nope, but I guess that would broaden my experience.'

'It will, though it's not just about experience; it also demonstrates your attitude. Early on in my career, I recall a colleague of mine who got into a role that she really wanted without having much experience simply by saying, "You can mould me in the way that you want. I'm willing to learn to do whatever you what want me to do." The last I heard, she's now running an overseas division of that company. I doubt that will work in every case, but her attitude shone through and I'm sure that made the difference.'

'As always, a lot of food for thought,' said Josh. 'If only I'd asked these questions sooner.'

'It's never too late to learn. Listen, I've got to go. But good luck.'

Josh made an extra effort, over the next few weeks, to maintain his performance at work despite his disappointment over the team leader role. However, he felt envious whenever he had to work with the new team leader. He began looking for volunteering opportunities outside work to develop his team-leading experience.

***

During week eighteen of the business squash league, Rory confirmed that Tomas and Josh would be playing the doubles games in weeks twenty-three and twenty-four. Tomas was the best player in the team and Josh was the only other player with experience of doubles matches from his university competitions.

Later that week, Josh was invited to an interview for a contract position as a marketing team leader. He'd put his CV on several career websites shortly after being turned down for the team leader role but had amended his current title to marketing team leader.

When they called him up, he lied that he had several months of team-leading experience as part of his role. He didn't think much of it and figured it was not going to go anywhere. He just wanted the experience of another interview.

He got a call the following Tuesday with an offer to start as soon as possible. The company was expanding and about to launch a few major campaigns, so it was looking for marketing team leaders to start as soon as possible.

That night, Josh burst into the flat really excited. Paul had only just arrived a minute or two earlier.

'I handed in my notice today.'

'What was that?' asked Paul.

'I said, "I handed in my notice today." I leave IM at the end of next week.'

He told Paul about the contract role. 'I wasn't expecting this,' said Josh. 'But I know that what I've been missing all this time is the freedom to control my own work.'

Paul was convinced Josh was just pulling his leg but then realised he was serious. 'You're kidding, right? Moving jobs again? Are you sure that's a wise move? I know it's not been all that you expected, but contracting is a huge risk to take.'

'I know. I can't explain it, but I just have this gut instinct that this is the right move. I feel excited,' said Josh.

'You do realise that could simply be because it's a change. Have you thought about what you'll do when the contract ends, especially if they don't extend it?'

'This is annoying. I'm finally choosing to think big and positive. Why do you have to put such a negative spin on it? Anyway, I've got enough saved up for three months.'

'You know I'm all for big and positive thinking. I just think you should also be realistic and consider the risks. Have you spoken to Tomas about it?'

'No. This is a decision that I've got to make for myself. Besides, he's an entrepreneur; he's bound to support my move. I'll tell him after I've made the move. Surprise him, I guess.'

'He'll be surprised all right. And Pete?' asked Paul.

'Not too impressed,' said Josh. 'He said he thought I was being a bit impatient with my development and impulsive with this move. Like I said, my gut says this is the right thing to do. Don't worry about me. I'm confident you won't have to say "I told you so" in a few months' time. It'll work out.'

'Well, if that's your decision, I'll be rooting for,' said Paul as he made his way to his room.

'Thanks.'

Paul turned back. 'Team leader, huh? And they weren't bothered that you didn't have any team-leading experience.'

'Not really,' said Josh as he looked away and turned on the TV.

***

During week twenty-two of the squash league, less than two weeks after starting with the new firm, Josh was called into the office of Pedro, the manager who had hired him.

'I'm afraid I've got bad news,' he said to Josh. 'You might want to sit down.'

Josh remained standing.

'Is everything OK with my work?' Only the night before he'd handed in some ideas for the marketing campaign he was working on.

'Your work is fine. That's not a problem.' Pedro paused. 'I wanted you to hear this directly from me. Unfortunately, two of the major projects we were bidding for have fallen through, and our parent company has gone into administration. It's going to be announced officially this afternoon.'

'Oh, no!'

Josh sat down slowly.

'I'm sorry to have to tell you this. I honestly wasn't aware of the situation when I took you on. Our division has been keeping the company afloat, but now even we're affected. I've been asked to reduce staff numbers and unfortunately that starts with non-permanent staff.'

'How long do I have?'

'Unfortunately, because you're still in the first month, it'll have to be no more than a week. I'm really sorry, Josh.'

Josh couldn't believe this was happening.

He thanked Pedro for letting him know and walked out of his office in a bit of a daze.

And things were going so well. Maybe Paul was right. I should have thought this through properly, he thought.

The rest of the week went by pretty quickly as Josh wrapped up his work on the campaign.

The following week, Josh and Tomas were meant to play the doubles match. He hadn't told Tomas about leaving IM or starting his new role, and now that he was out of work, he couldn't bear to face him. He sent a message to Tomas and Rory via Sheree to say that he was sick and wouldn't be able to play any of the upcoming matches.

Tomas and Rory called back on Monday morning and left messages on his phone, but Josh didn't return any of their messages.

I can't believe I'm doing this, he thought while ignoring a call from TWC.

Summary of Principles and Lessons

If I want to progress to the next level, I need to begin operating at that level long before I'm officially there.

By taking initiative, I can get the right experience that will help me gain new skills and knowledge.

Employers and managers are always looking for individuals who show initiative.

Consider shadowing or volunteering for opportunities to gain new skills and experiences.

There are so many opportunities in my organisation to gain experience and skills above and beyond what I normally would.

Developing the skills I need for the next level isn't an excuse to drop the ball in my current role.

To get out of a catch-22, I should have a great attitude, deliver well, maintain a lot of great relationships, and get as much exposure as possible, even if that means trying a few things when the opportunities come up.

8—Face Up to Your Fears

Don't waste life in doubts and fears; spend yourself on the work before you, well assured that the right performance of this hour's duties will be the best preparation for the hours or ages that follow it.

—Ralph Waldo Emerson

Over the next four months, Josh only had three interviews despite sending out hundreds of CVs. One company invited him to the second stage of the interview and then called to cancel it a few days before. They said that senior management wanted the job filled by an internal candidate to promote staff progression.

Paul and Tim had recently offered to help cover his rent for a time while he worked at securing a job. His mum had also loaned him some money, even though Josh hated taking money from her. He felt it should be the other way 'round by now.

One Thursday evening, three months after the business squash league had ended, Paul walked into the flat just as Josh was getting off the phone.

'That was my mum, again! She's called me almost every day over the last three weeks to see if I've gotten a job. You'd think these things come easy. I'm feeling depressed enough as it is.'

'Well, I guess that's a good lesson for you,' muttered Paul. The words came out before he could take them back.

'What's that supposed to mean? Do you think I'm not taking this seriously? For your information, I am!'

'Look, Josh, I'm going to be straight with you. For some reason, and I say this as a friend, you're just not the sort of person who's willing to do whatever it takes to make something work out. As soon as the heat is turned up, you slack off. Don't get me wrong, you're a great friend. It's just that your attitude sucks! You've always come across like you expect life to be easy and give you great rewards for so little effort. You were exactly the same at uni. Tim and I are more than happy to help out. We're just not sure you're going to do all that you need to.'

'What? I can't believe you're saying this. And who are you to talk anyway? Your parents can buy you anything you want. You could work in your dad's law firm if you were ever out of work. So it's not like you ever have anything to worry about. As for Tim—'

'You don't get it, do you?' said Paul.

'Get what?'

'Yeah, you're right. I could've chosen to work for my dad. And I still get treated like a bit of a rebel for choosing a different path when everything was laid out for me. But, believe it or not, having everything laid out for me put even more pressure on me. Growing up, I wasn't exactly the smartest kid on the block. I remember getting teased by some of the other boys in my class. They used to call me the dumb, rich kid. I didn't like that. When I told my parents, they just said not to worry about it because I was smart in their eyes, and besides, I was being groomed for the family business so I was bound to be successful. That made me so much more determined to succeed on my own, even if that meant being in my dad's black books for a while. I often wish I had your intelligence or some of your strengths, yet you are just so complacent. You never want to give a hundred percent to anything if it's not what *you* want to do. It's as if you're afraid that your best won't be good enough. You know what, all the advice in the world, even from Tomas who I have incredible respect for, won't count for anything if you don't change your attitude. It's time to grow up!'

'You have no idea what you're talking about!' snapped Josh.

'Maybe, but I'm telling you what I've seen over the—'

'I don't have to listen to this,' interrupted Josh as he walked out of the house and slammed the door.

***

For more than a week, Josh avoided Paul like the plague.

On Saturday morning, Paul was just about to head out when Josh came into the hallway.

'Have you a got a minute?' Josh asked.

Paul looked at his watch and slowly nodded.

They sat down in the living room on opposite sides.

Paul spoke up. 'Actually, J, before you say anything, about the other week, maybe some of the things I said were a bit harsh.'

'Seriously, Paul, don't apologise. You were totally right. I think that's what made it even harder to hear. Everything you said cut me like a doctor's knife.'

'Scalpel.'

'Huh? Oh, yeah, whatever. Listen, I've been doing a lot of soul-searching over the past week, and it hasn't been pleasant. When you said I come across like I'm never willing to give a hundred percent and I'm afraid my best wouldn't be good enough or something, it clicked for me. You're totally right. I am afraid, and my attitude does suck!'

'That just came out. It wasn't like—'

'It's OK. Hear me out. I'm afraid of how bad I would feel if I gave my best but still didn't get the outcome I wanted. I think that's what happened at IM. I was getting all this good advice and thought I was doing all the right things, so when the team leader role came up, I felt certain I was going to get it. But when it didn't happen, I was devastated. As soon as another opportunity came up, I took it. Maybe I felt I deserved the break and that IM had blown their chance of keeping me. In a way, I've been pursuing success on my terms. And if I'd been honest, I shouldn't have got that job anyway.'

Paul looked surprised. 'Why's that?'

Josh told him about the lie.

'J! How could you? That could have so backfired in your face. You're really lucky that they had to let you go before they figured that out.'

'Yeah, I know. I don't know what I was thinking. It was stupid of me, to be honest.'

'Really stupid.'

'I know, I know. Listen, over the last few days I realised that for a long time I've been sabotaging my chances of success by my own attitude and behaviour.'

'What do you mean?'

'Well, you know I told you I went to an international secondary school.'

'Yeah …'

'Well, I don't think I ever told you that I was top of my entire class for the first three years, but something changed during my fourth year. We suddenly had to choose our core subjects in preparation for our finals, and since I was dead set on becoming a doctor, I focused on the sciences and actually dropped some of the other subjects that I excelled in, like music and French.'

'OK?' said Paul, unsure of where this was going.

'Well, after that my grades dropped. I still averaged over seventy percent, but I was no longer one of the top students in my class. Now, the truth is that up until then I'd been relying mostly on raw talent and intellect. I worked hard during exams, but not that hard, and so when I dropped my stronger subjects it showed.'

'Wow. I guess you couldn't really know at the time,' said Paul.

'You're right. I didn't know what was going on at the time. I just know that I felt embarrassed, disappointed, and afraid that maybe I didn't have what it took to be a doctor after all. Maybe I wasn't actually that smart. I felt overwhelmed with all these doubts, fears, and insecurities. Looking back now, I just wish someone had told me that I needed to work harder or something. Anyway, I sort of made this unconscious decision not to give one hundred percent because I was afraid it would never be enough. At least that way, I could always feel good about myself.'

'How's that?'

'Well, I guess I felt that if I only put in a little effort and got great results, I could tell myself it was because I was smart. But if I didn't get great results, I could tell myself it was because I hadn't given a hundred percent effort. So either way I could win. At least, that's what I convinced myself.'

'Man! That is some silly logic,' said Paul.

'Now you tell me. I never realised that my version of winning was actually more like self-sabotage.'

They were both silent.

After a while, Paul said, 'I'm not really sure what to say. I guess it's great that you've figured this stuff out. Better late than never, they say.'

'I hope so,' said Josh.

'You know, one of the things I realised in dealing with my dad and the whole career choice situation was that our fears so often blow little events or anticipated challenges out of proportion. So much so that, in our minds, a light, breezy wind turns into a life-threatening hurricane with huge hail storms to boot. The secret was in confronting my fears head-on.'

'Sounds like something Tomas would say,' said Josh.

'Well, he probably did say something that helped me during that time. I know he certainly helped Dad get some perspective. Anyway, what I'm trying to say is that if I had given in to my fears, I'd probably be an extremely wealthy and miserable lawyer.'

Josh smiled.

'So where to from here?' asked Paul.

'I've been thinking about that.'

Josh told Paul about his plan.

'Wow! Are you sure you're up for that?' quizzed Paul.

'I think so.'

'OK. Good luck!' Paul looked up at the clock. 'Oh, no! Look at the time. I've got to run. Jaz will be waiting for me. We're checking out decorations and flowers for the church and hall.'

'Oh, yeah. Sorry. Tell Jaz it was my fault.'

'Trust me: I will.'

Paul sprinted for the front door.

As he was about to close, Josh shouted out, 'Hey, Paul!'

Paul poked his head 'round the door.

'Yup.'

'Thanks for listening, and I'm sorry I took it out on you the other day. It was just—'

'Hey, don't worry. I've really got to go. Just make sure your plan works.'

Josh nodded and smiled.

Summary of Principles and Lessons

Our fears so often blow little events and anticipated challenges out of proportion and cause us to sabotage our own path to success.

The secret to overcoming our fears, doubts, and insecurities, and the huge storms they create, is in confronting them head-on.

9—Adopt a Winning Attitude

A great attitude does much more than turn on the lights
in our worlds; it seems to magically connect us to all sorts
of serendipitous opportunities that were somehow absent
before the change.

—Earl Nightingale

As Josh stepped out of the lift, he realised that it had been more than five months since he had seen Tomas.

When he put his plan in motion, he wasn't sure how Tomas or the others would respond, and this time he wasn't going to let that stop him. He just knew it was the right thing to do. He'd asked both Paul and Tim to comment on all of the letters before sending them off.

Rory called him up a few days afterwards and gave him an earful for burying his head in the sand. 'Tomas doesn't take lightly to poor team players,' he'd said. 'But, by the sounds of it, I think you've learnt a valuable lesson, so I won't go on. You've actually shown a lot of guts by taking this step, so well done!'

Later that same day, less than a few hours after Rory's call, Josh received emails from Finn, Ola, and Toby, each thanking him for their letter and suggesting they meet up for drinks soon. He was surprised but grateful for their responses.

The call from Sheree came about a week after sending the letters. Tomas had asked her to schedule an appointment for Josh to come in and see him. He was going on a family holiday for two weeks, so the earliest he'd be free to see Josh was the Tuesday morning after he got back.

On his way to Tomas's office, Josh had reread the letter he'd sent him.

Dear Tomas,

First of all, I owe you, Rory, Finn, Ola, and Toby a massive apology. I'm extremely sorry that when things got difficult for me, I let that affect my commitment to the team and let you all down. Just so you know, I've written an apology note to all the others as well.

I must say, I was glad to hear that team TWC came second in the league. Maybe my absence was good luck.

On a more serious note, I feel that I particularly owe you a full explanation for what happened. I didn't realise how much not getting the team leader role at IM affected me, but a few weeks later, I was offered a contract role with Towers Media Group as a marketing team leader. It's a long story, but they only offered me the role because I lied about my experience. It was stupid of me, I know, but I took it. I guess I felt that IM weren't delivering and so I needed to go elsewhere.

Unfortunately, Towers Media Group had to let me go only two weeks after joining them because the parent company was having financial problems. I obviously hadn't done adequate research on them before saying yes. It was only afterward I found out that the division that had hired me was the only profitable part of the company in the last two years.

I should have said something sooner, but I felt too ashamed to let you know what had happened, especially because of all the excellent advice you'd given me over the last six months and the people you'd introduced me to. I just felt I'd blown it big time, so I lied to you and Rory that I was too sick to continue with the squash league. I couldn't muster the courage to face you, so I just let it get the better of me, and it's taken me a while to pick myself up. Paul and I even had a bust-up recently about my attitude.

Reflecting on my time at IM, I think that most of the changes I'd been making were so that I could get the outcome I wanted and not, as you often said, so that I could develop a strong and resilient character. I didn't really want to be like the caterpillar. I wanted success on my own terms and in my own time.

Anyway, I've finally realised what all this talk about having the right attitude really means for me. It's about giving my best and doing what needs to be done in every situation, whether I feel like it or not, and not letting the fear of failure hold me back. It's a shame it's taken me this long to figure that out.

Once again, I'm really sorry that I let the team down. And I'm even sorrier that I let you down, especially since you showed faith in me by allowing me to be part of Team TWC and investing time in me since our first meeting. I'm truly sorry.

If it's OK with you, I'd also like to apologise in person, but I understand if you think otherwise.

Yours sincerely,
Josh

'I'm glad I swallowed my pride and sent this.'

Tomas was just getting off the phone as Josh entered his office. 'Hi, Tomas.'

'Hi, Josh. It's been a while.'

'Yes it has. Thanks for agreeing to see me again.' Josh quickly added, 'How was your holiday?'

'It was excellent! Thanks for asking. Every year, around about this time, I take my family on a sailing holiday. We've been doing it for about five years now. This time we explored the coastline of Croatia from a town called Zadar all the way down to Dubrovnik. Have you ever been to Croatia?'

'Nope, but I hear it's beautiful.'

'Oh, yes. It's got more than three thousand kilometres of coastline with something like seven hundred islands and lots of hidden bays, beaches, cliffs, and fantastic diving opportunities. My wife and the kids had a great time.'

'Sounds really nice. I can imagine the weather was great.'

'Oh, it definitely was. That part of the coastline is one of the sunniest in all of Europe, which is one of the reasons we chose it. It's definitely worth a visit.'

'I've got a list of must-sees. I'll have to add Croatia to it.'

Tomas smiled and reached for his leather folder.

'So, I see a lot has been happening in your life lately. Thanks for your letter.'

'Honestly, I wasn't sure how you would respond and, like I said, I really wanted to apologise in person as well. Maybe things would have been different if I'd been upfront sooner, but I was really embarrassed and annoyed with myself. Anyway, I'm sorry that I let the team down. And more so that I let you down, especially considering how much you've gone out of your way for me. I have really valued all your advice. As difficult as this has been, I'm sort of glad it happened because there's no more hiding. It's actually helped me see myself and my attitudes more clearly.'

'Well, I think you've shown a lot of courage in owning up, taking responsibility, and apologising to me and the others, so apology accepted.'

Josh thanked Tomas and went on to tell him about his argument with Paul.

'After that I spent a few days sulking, but it became clear to me that he was right and that if I was ever going to make the most of all the advice I'd been given, then I really needed to change my attitude and self-sabotaging behaviour. So now I'm determined to adopt the attitude of giving my best, whatever the circumstances.'

'Sounds like a major breakthrough for you,' said Tomas.

'Yeah, I really think so.'

'And that attitude you talk about is one I often refer to as a winning attitude. I like to define it this way: a way of thinking that empowers you to wholeheartedly and resolutely give the best of who you are—skills, talents, experience, and passion—right here, right now. After all, that's all you can really control. And the critical thing is that it's not determined or influenced by results or outcomes; it's about character. It's about who you are.'

'It sounds even more inspiring that way. But, yes, that pretty much sums it. Whatever circumstances I find myself in, I can choose to have a winning attitude! I just wish someone had told me that sooner.'

'I don't think it would have made much of a difference until you saw for yourself how damaging some of your existing actions, beliefs, and behaviours really were. Our attitudes are based on our deep-seated beliefs. In your case, you needed to change your beliefs in order to change your attitude. And that takes time and a good degree of self-awareness.'

'Yeah, I guess you're right.'

'The good thing is you didn't give up. Well, not completely. I must admit, I wasn't impressed with your attitude when we first met. I could've easily given you a job or spoken to someone I know, but you didn't have the right attitude. However, I did sense a genuine desire within you to make your life count for something, which is why I decided to make myself available.'

'It's a shame I blew it.'

'It may feel like that, but in the grand scheme of things you haven't blown it. You should actually be proud of yourself.'

'You think so?'

'Absolutely! A lot of people don't push through to learn the lessons that you're learning, and then they wonder why they never have a sense of peace and fulfilment in their work,' said Tomas.

'Hmmm ...'

'By the way, you mentioned in your letter that you lied about your experience to get the job with Towers Media Group. What was that about?'

Josh nodded slowly. 'Yeah, that was a silly, silly mistake. I really regret doing that. It was another case of trying to get somewhere before I was ready.'

'I think you sound broken enough about it, so I won't dwell on it for too long other than to say I've learnt that it's essential that you always do what's right no matter what you think the consequences will be. Otherwise, you'll end up compromising your integrity and building your life on a lie. I believe that if you're true to yourself and maintain your integrity, even if you fail or things don't work out as you planned, you can still hold your head up high and be proud of yourself, and that's something you should always hold on to.'

'That's really helpful to hear. And I appreciate your bringing that up,' said Josh.

'Enough said then. So how's the job hunting going?'

'Not too good. I've sent out hundreds of CVs, but I haven't landed anything yet, though I have had a few interviews. Pete did say I could always come back to IM, but I think that's because of my sister. I feel bad that I didn't do that much research on Towers Media Group before saying yes. Not that I should have got it anyway. Actually, I didn't do that much planning at all before I gave in my notice at IM. I just had this gut instinct that it was the right thing to do. Is it so wrong to follow your instincts?'

'I think instincts are important. I certainly follow mine and often find that they are correct. However, I think it's dangerous to rely on them alone. You need to know how and when to use evidence strategically.'

'You mean test your instincts?'

'Yes. They need to be tempered with whatever information is available to you. Otherwise, you'll end up doing everything on a whim.'

'That sounds like me all right.'

'You're not alone. Early on in my business, I made many strategic decisions based on gut feeling, and that got me into trouble. I soon learnt that, although instincts are important, they are honed and refined through experience, learning, and knowledge. So now, even if it seems my instincts are often right, I still check most of my major strategic decisions with my senior team.'

'Does that mean I've got a long way to go before I can trust my instincts?' asked Josh.

'I think you should always pay attention to your instincts. At the same time, it's important to develop a mature sense of the limitations of your own judgement. For example, when thinking about joining a company, I'd say you need to be analytical and do your research, but when thinking about the specifics of a role you need to use a good mix of instincts and some analysis. You've got to know when to use your head and when to use your heart, which isn't always easy.'

'But if something feels wrong, surely that means it is?' said Josh.

'It depends. If something feels wrong, it may very well mean something isn't right, but you should still look very hard at the issue and talk to others. I don't think there is any substitute for consulting widely and tempering your instincts with wisdom, especially at your stage in your career.'

'As good as this is to hear, and despite all that I've learnt recently, I still feel like a failure. It's been more than four months now and I still haven't found anything. I've made a big mistake and don't really know how to turn it around.'

'Everyone makes mistakes. I've made loads.'

'Yes, but you've probably never made a massive mistake that could just about end your career or business.'

'The only reason that I'm running a successful business now is because of all the mistakes that I've made, and I'm sure I'll make more in the future. I'm a strong believer in the fact that every time you make a mistake, you get much more valuable feedback and wisdom than if you did nothing at all. I don't regret making any of the mistakes that I made. I'd say the most significant one nearly sent me into bankruptcy about eight years ago.'

'Was that when you said you almost had to sell your house?'

'Yes, I made the wrong choice of business partner, and his lack of integrity meant that a significant amount of our company funds were misused. I'd seen the signs but just chose to ignore them. When I realised what was going on, I had to buy him out, and it took almost a year to recover, but as Thomas Edison once said, "The best way to recover from mistakes is to celebrate them because you've just become more experienced."'

'That's a good one.'

'When it comes to making mistakes, it's not that those who succeed don't make mistakes. They've simply learnt to get up each time and assess why they fell in the first place so it doesn't happen again. Some of the most successful people

I know have made some of the biggest mistakes. And now they couldn't put a price tag on the experience they gained. You should speak to Martin and Sonya. They've got quite a story to tell.'

'I will.' Josh made a note on his iPad. 'So does this mean I can arrange to meet up with you again?'

'Only if you promise not to go AWOL.'

They both laughed.

***

Josh hadn't been in touch with Martin or Sonya for several months. Although he still felt a bit embarrassed about his situation, his time with Tomas had put him at ease about discussing it with them.

He sent them an email with a brief summary of recent events and about Tomas's suggestion to speak with them.

Sonya sent a reply asking Josh to liaise with her PA for a suitable time to talk. Sonya's PA, Merle, called Josh and confirmed a phone appointment for 3 p.m. on Friday.

Josh called on the day and spoke to Merle who then put him through to Sonya.

'Hi, Josh,' Sonya said. 'Thanks for your email. I heard you couldn't continue with the league, but Tomas didn't say why. It became clear when I received your email.'

'Yeah, I wasn't exactly full of enthusiasm about what had happened. It felt like I had wasted all that time and not listened to a word of advice I'd been given by any of you. I made a big mistake that could have been easily avoided.'

'Well, that's life for you. Even with the best advice in the world, you're still going to make mistakes. As a good friend of mine always says, "You've got to fall off a horse in order to ride properly."'

'I'm beginning to realise that now. Have you ever come close to making a career-ending mistake?'

'I wouldn't describe your situation as career ending but, yes, I can think of a few personally. One that stands out to me was just after I made the switch from criminal to corporate law. I was in my late twenties, doing really well, and had just been headhunted to work for a large mining company as their head of legal affairs. I was responsible for a budget of about fifty million pounds. During my first two years, I remember working harder than everyone around me. It was as though I was trying to prove myself as the top performer and superstar everyone thought I was. Unfortunately, it wasn't sustainable and I almost had a nervous breakdown.'

'Wow! I wouldn't have guessed.'

'Well, I knew I had a problem when I approved a settlement for five million pounds when it should have been for five hundred thousand. I had taken on so much and was so exhausted that I was dropping the ball in a few key areas.'

'How did you turn it around?'

'Simple. Humility.'

'Humility?'

'That's what it took for me: humility. Humility to ask for help and to realise that I'm human and needed to pace myself as such. I believe you can avoid a lot of mistakes by not letting pride get the best of you. I also got help in restructuring my team. People are usually willing to help if you admit you've made a mistake.'

'I've definitely been guilty of not asking for help quickly. I guess I just thought I should be able to figure out a lot of things myself. Now I realise that I'm missing out on an opportunity to learn, especially if I don't know what I don't know. I'm wondering though, have you ever been in a role that you thought was a mistake?'

'Not that I can think of. Maybe the reason for that is I've always had a clear understanding of the purpose of any role before saying yes to it and taking it on. However, I do recall being in one role longer than I should have.'

'What did you do?'

'I negotiated a significant pay rise in my last year with that organisation. So by the time I left, I was able to secure a very good deal—even though I had stayed in the role longer than I felt necessary for development purposes. It's important that you learn to capitalise on any experience, good or bad.'

'So there's always something good that can come out of any situation, you think?'

'Sometimes, it could be as simple as learning something new about yourself.'

'Up until now, I haven't realised how important self-awareness is. Anyway, I should let you get back to work. Thanks very much for your time.'

'You're welcome. Remember that if you are willing and eager to learn, you are more useful to any organisation that wants to develop you.'

'Thanks. I'll be sure not to forget that.'

'Don't. Oh, and good luck with the job hunting. By the way, what are you looking for exactly?'

'Something in marketing, I guess.'

'OK. If I hear of anything specific, I'll let you know. In the meantime, send me a copy of your CV.'

'I will do. Thanks very much.'

After the call, as Josh made a few notes, he noticed he'd received an email from Martin's PA, Becky. Martin was free to speak at 6 p.m. that evening.

At 5.30 p.m., Josh received a call from Martin's office. He needed to leave earlier than planned but was able to squeeze in the call if Josh was available to talk. Otherwise, it would have to be rescheduled for a later date.

Josh said he was able to take the call now.

'Hi, Josh,' said Martin. 'I see you got yourself into a bit of a pickle.'

'I'm afraid so. It feels like more than a pickle. I guess my ambitions got ahead of me.'

'I know that feeling,' said Martin.

'It's a surprise to know you've made serious mistakes in your career and still gotten to where you are today.'

'No one's above making serious mistakes. Remember I told you that I started off as an engineer and then caught the management bug?'

'Yeah, I remember that,' said Josh, nodding even though Martin couldn't see him.

'Well, as soon as I realised that my forte was dealing with people and business development, I focused on management and got promoted very quickly. However, it was probably too fast too soon. About fifteen years ago, I took on a job as divisional director for one of our group divisions. At the time, it was probably one job too big. I instantly knew that I'd gone a step too far, but I wanted the job so much that I didn't really consider whether or not I could actually do it. I soon realised that I didn't have a broad enough experience to do the role effectively. It took me six months to own up to my boss and others around me.

'When I finally did, the reaction was surprising. My boss was very supportive, even though they had to bring in three people to support the management structure. But I learnt so much from them. That was one of the best things that has ever happened in my career even though it began with a major mistake on my part,' said Martin.

'Sounds like your decision to be humble made the difference in turning it around,' said Josh, thinking of his conversation with Sonya.

'Yes, that and being self-aware, honest with myself, and having trusted people around me. There have been other occasions over the years where I've shown poor judgement. But I must say, especially looking back, that every experience has been useful. It's healthy and natural to make mistakes because you can learn a lot about yourself. If you let it, those situations can help shape your character for the better.'

'I wish it was that easy for me to just laugh at a mistake and move on. Sometimes, I can be so hard on myself for making mistakes rather than learn from them quickly,' said Josh.

'No one is saying you've got to enjoy your mistakes, because they can often be very painful. And I say that from personal experience. But you've got to accept the fact that making mistakes is only natural. Whatever you do, don't get hung up on your mistakes. Learn from them. Life can be over very quickly, so don't wish experiences away, even the bad stuff.'

'I need to keep reminding myself that. Thanks very much.'

'You're welcome. By the way, I don't know if Tomas has mentioned this already, but in just more than two weeks, on Saturday, he and I are organising a charity breakfast event for the youth charity that we're on the board of. You're welcome to come along to that if you want. It'll be a good opportunity to support the charity and meet lots of people.'

'Sounds great. Yes, please count me in.'

'Good. I'll ask Becky to send you details.'

Josh sent an email to Tomas later that day with an update of his conversations with Martin and Sonya.

Summary of Principles and Lessons

A winning attitude is about wholeheartedly and resolutely doing the best I can with all I have—skills, talents, and experience—right here, right now. After all, that's all I can control.

If I'm true to myself and maintain my integrity, then I can always hold my head up high regardless of how things turn out.

Instincts are important, but it's dangerous for me to rely on them solely as they are refined through experience, learning, and knowledge.

There's no substitute for consulting widely and tempering my instincts with wisdom.

Even with the best advice in the world, I'm still going to make mistakes—it's natural!

I should always be humble enough to own up to my mistakes and get help—People are usually willing to help if I own up.

I should learn to capitalise on any experience, good or bad.

Don't get hung up on my mistakes. Learn from them, and let the situation help shape my character for the better.

Life can be over very quickly, so I shouldn't wish experiences away.

10—Develop a Winning Focus

He is a wise man who wastes no energy on pursuits for which he is not fitted; and he is still wiser who, among the things that he can do well, chooses and resolutely follows the best.

–William Ewart Gladstone

'Where are you off to this early in the morning?' asked Paul. It was 7.30 on Saturday.

'I'm off to a charity breakfast event that Tomas is co-organising.'

'Oh, I heard about that. I think Mum and Dad are going be there. Jaz and I are meeting up later this morning to do some wedding planning. I hope you're still planning to meet us and the other guys this afternoon to try out the tuxes?'

It was more than six months to the wedding, but Paul and Jaz had already sorted out most of the details, except for bridal party dresses and the men's suits. And that was only because it had taken a while to agree on a colour scheme they were both happy with.

'Oh, shoot!'

'J!'

'I'm just kidding. Yep, I'll be there.'

***

There were a lot of people at the breakfast event. Josh saw Paul's parents at a table next to Tomas's. He went over and chatted with them for a while. He mentioned that he was meeting up with Paul afterwards to pick out the groomsmen suits.

Afterwards, as he mingled, he bumped into Paula, the non-executive director of the insurance company. He hadn't seen her since the European Business Leaders Convention. She was on the board of trustees of the youth charity, along with Tomas and Martin. She recognised Josh's face but had forgotten his name.

'Ah, yes, Josh. Good to see you again. How's it going?' she asked.

Josh was about to offer his usual, 'Fine thanks.' But instead, he said, 'Well, to be honest, it's been a difficult few months. I lost my job and have been trying to get a new one.'

He told Paula about recent events, his conversations with Paul and Tomas, and his realisation that his attitude, fears, and doubts had held him back for so long.

As Josh concluded, he said, 'I'm determined to get something, anything, and just give my best.' He paused for a few seconds and then said, 'I have wondered though what happens to the person who goes to work, has a winning attitude, and does what is required and more, but still finds himself getting nowhere.'

'That's easy,' said Paula. 'It usually means they're not working in the area of their core strengths.'

'What do you mean?'

'Well, I believe that everybody has a unique arena in which they can flourish and a responsibility to find out what that is. It doesn't have to mean a change of jobs, but the right role for you will be one that plays to your core strengths. I spend some of my time advising emerging companies that have customer-facing staff, and I often say that if you can get your people to have a winning focus and love what they do, your customer will love what you do!'

'Isn't it difficult getting people to actually love what they do?'

'Well, that's where the winning focus comes in. A big part of getting people to love and excel in what they do is helping them figure out who they are, such as knowing their strengths, weaknesses, passions, and values. Once they know what their strengths are, the key is to focus on doing everything they can to use those strengths as often as possible so that they develop, grow, and shine. I always find that it's a win-win for the individuals and the organisation.'

'Wow! That's very interesting. Growing up, all I wanted was to become a doctor, so when that didn't work out I just followed a path that I thought made sense. I've never really found a passion for a specific career since then, but whenever I see people excelling in a specific role or career, I get jealous. Sometimes, I think I should be doing whatever they're doing. So far it's felt like I've been living someone else's life,' said Josh.

'A good friend of mine once said to me, "No one has on their tombstone that he was better than his brother or he was worse than his brother. No one's obituary compares them with others." I think she was spot on. You're remembered for what you contributed rather than how you compared. Yet somehow, most of life seems to be about comparisons, and that drives our view about work and job. If you really want to succeed, don't compare yourself with others. Instead, focus on discovering your strengths and maximising your contribution to the world.'

'It's so easy to compare, though,' said Josh.

'Of course it is. And I've seen so many people and companies fail because they're too focused on following in the footsteps of others and being what they're not instead of focusing on being the best that they could be with the skills, talents, abilities, and resources they have.'

'Maybe that's why I've been feeling so uncomfortable these last few years,' said Josh. 'I've liked all the people that I've worked with—well, most of them—and I'm quite sociable, which is probably why I've done OK in my jobs. But I've never really enjoyed them. I know I haven't always had the right attitude and given my best, but now I really want to do something that I'm passionate about and that I believe in.'

'Having a passion for what you do is contagious. It's what will drive you to develop the skills you need to succeed. It's what will keep your spirit up, even when the going is tough. It's what will compel you to put in the hard work and develop mastery, which in turn builds confidence.'

'This is so inspiring! I wish I had figured this out years ago. At least, before I started working.'

'It's not always that simple. Discovering who you are is a journey rather than a one-time event. Often through trial and error, we begin to realise our preferences for working styles, our strengths and weaknesses, and what really gets us excited. The problem is that very few people take the time to look within and ask questions about their passions and values and how that relates to the world of work. Think about it. Have you ever taken the time to really understand what you're about as a person, your purpose in life and what you like or dislike about the world of work?'

'Not until recently, I guess,' said Josh. 'Most of the time I've just complained and got on with it, or quit. Recently, I thought I just need to work on my weak areas.'

'I think it's a very poor strategy to try and develop your weaknesses whilst coasting on your strengths. You don't have time to do it all, so you might as well focus on your strengths. If your goal is to become good at everything, you'll end up being average at most things.'

Josh suddenly remembered the piece of paper Tomas had given him when they first met, and he almost kicked himself. 'Actually, I think I have something that might get me off to a good start.'

He told Paula about some of the questions on the piece of paper from Tomas.

'That's exactly what I'm talking about,' she said. 'It'll take a while to work through, but it will pay dividends.'

'I can't wait to get started on this.'

'Well, good luck with it.'

Looking at his watch, Josh noticed that it was 11.30 a.m. It would take him twenty-five minutes to get to the tuxedo shops.

'Better not be late. Thanks for your time and advice, Paula.'

Josh said goodbye to Tomas, Martin, and Paul's parents. He had a spring in his step as he made his way out of the hall.

***

Later that evening, Josh looked for the paper with the list of questions that Tomas had given him. He typed them into his iPad and spent several days thinking through and answering the questions.

The following week, he was on the phone with Tomas. He told him about his conversation with Paula and that he'd started working through the questions that Tomas gave him when they first met.

'I've still got some way to go,' said Josh. 'But it's been a very useful exercise so far. My only regret is that I didn't pay attention to this when you first gave it to me. It would have saved me a lot of grief. Then again, I probably wasn't ready. I certainly didn't have the right attitude then. By the way, one of the questions asks about my weaknesses. If I'm meant to focus on my strengths, why do I need to identify my weaknesses?'

'That's a good question. Identifying your strengths is critical and is what lays the foundation for excelling in your career, yet so many people are often more conscious of what their weaknesses are. However, identifying your weaknesses helps you know what to avoid, so you can focus on building and leveraging your strengths.'

'I see. So how do I actually build on and leverage my strengths?'

'Well, you've actually got to know what they are; otherwise, you won't be able to leverage them effectively.'

'And how do you do that? How do you *really* know them?'

'Well, there are several things you can do. You need to pay attention to what you do really well. The questions you've started working through are a fantastic start. They'll help raise your awareness of what your strengths and weaknesses are, as well as what you enjoy doing—and equally important, what you don't enjoy doing. The other important element is paying attention to the verbal and non-verbal feedback you receive.'

'Feedback?'

'Yes, feedback is extremely valuable. We see this all the time in sports. The best sports people have coaches and get direct, real-time feedback on what they are doing well and where they need to develop.'

'So you mean getting feedback from others around you, like a manager, colleagues?' asked Josh.

'Yes. If understanding your strengths and weaknesses is one of the most important things you can do early on in your career, and I believe it is, then getting feedback from others is one of the ways you can do that, especially those around with you more experience.'

'I know a lot of people who don't enjoy sitting down with their bosses, especially to hear what they could do even better. I never enjoyed it.'

'There's a big difference between valuing something and enjoying it. I'm not saying that everyone who gives feedback is particularly skilled at it. Giving good and effective feedback is a skill that needs to be learnt and developed. And maybe a lot of the people you're referring to have managers who need to develop that skill. But from your point of view, you've got to be focused on receiving the gold nuggets in whatever feedback you are given. Inner honesty is critical to success, and feedback helps you develop that. However, you've also got to remember that verbal feedback is only one part of it. We also get non-verbal feedback from the results of our work.'

'You mean how well I'm actually performing in any given task?'

'Precisely! The world gives you lots of feedback, even if people don't do it directly. For example, if you're in sales, you don't need to wait to see your boss before you get feedback on how you're doing.'

Josh was silent as he made a few notes on his iPad.

Then he asked, 'Are there any other ways that I could learn about my strengths?'

'Sometimes it takes good old-fashioned trial and error. You'll find that your strengths emerge as you become attracted to the things that you're really good at it. This means you've got to be willing to take risks, even if you think it might highlight your weaknesses, because whatever the case may be, it's an opportunity to gain a good understanding of yourself. For example, I like the idea that tennis players test themselves on more than one surface so that they gain a really good picture of what they can do and what their strengths and weaknesses are. So, don't be afraid to test yourself in more than one environment.'

'This is really helpful. I'll let you know how I get on. I still have this niggling fear of the unknown. What if this reveals something that is way too scary for me to do?'

'Living out who you are and being the person you know you're meant to be is no mean feat. It always involves confronting your fears. And fear of failure is probably the biggest obstacle to overcome. Let's discuss your answers when next we meet.'

'That would be great.'

***

Josh decided to review some of his questions with others and get feedback from them, so he spoke with Paul, Tim, his mum, and Leesa, and he even called IM to speak with Lewis and Pete. Pete said the offer of a job was still open. Josh decided not to rush into a decision. He said he would think about it.

He found a few old performance review reports and looked through them.

As he continued to work through the questions and consider the feedback from others, an interesting picture emerged.

***

When Josh met up with Tomas, he was so eager to talk through the questions and his answers. He had printed out a copy for Tomas.

They went on to talk through Josh's responses to each of the questions, and Tomas quizzed him on some of his responses.

What are your core values? What's important to you?

Achievement, advancement, ambition, care, contribution, effectiveness, enjoyment, freedom, impact, making a difference, persuasiveness, satisfaction, service to others, teamwork, and variety.

What needs are you most drawn to in the world or in your local community?

Improving people's lives, especially where they have been affected by illness. This might be because of my dad's death. I also enjoy the idea of working with young people, possibly because I didn't grow up with my dad.

Taking into account all areas of your life—physical, emotional, spiritual, professional, and social—what sort of lifestyle do you want?'

A great degree of flexibility and autonomy with my work. A job that plays to my strengths and involves lots of interactions with people.
To earn enough to help my mum retire comfortably in a few years.

What sort of person do you want to be?

I want to be someone who makes a difference in the life of others. I don't particularly enjoy chemistry or biology, so I know that medicine isn't for me anymore, but I wouldn't rule out some sort of work linked to the health-care industry.

What aspects of your current/most recent job do you like most?

I loved interacting with clients and exploring ideas. I didn't like the research calls, but I really enjoyed the sales calls.

What aspects of your current/most recent job do you like least?

At IM, I hated doing the desktop and online research. Maybe it was because it meant very little interaction with others. I loved being around people, especially our clients.

What would others say are your top strengths?

Ability to quickly build rapport and create a connection with people from all backgrounds.

When I believe in something, I speak passionately about it in a way that is very convincing.

A strong communicator.

A strong ability to examine, investigate, and evaluate information.

Creative facilitator of ideas and solutions to address a problem.

What would others say are your top areas for improvement?

I get bored very easily if I don't enjoy something, and it shows in my body language and my communication; I need to learn to stick to things and see them through regardless of how I feel; I need to do my work to a high standard all the time

What main skills do you enjoy using most?

Debating.

I enjoy and am good at sharing ideas and imparting information (communicating).

I enjoy and am good at convincing people with an argument when I'm passionate about the subject (promoting).

I enjoy and am good at assisting others (serving).

I enjoy and am good at shaping ideas and trying to change people's minds if I believe in something (influencing).

What do you enjoy doing in your free time for fun? For relaxation?

Crossword puzzles, socialising with friends, travelling, and watching foreign-language films and medical documentaries

If someone were writing a play about the highlights of your life, what would be included (past, present, and future events)?

The debating competitions I won in secondary school (past).
Highlights of the countries I've travelled to (past).
People that I've helped through my charity work (future).

'Well done. It looks like you've put a lot of thought into this.'

'I got a lot of feedback which really helped.'

No one had ever spoken to Josh in detail about his talents, passions, or skills like this before. It was an exciting new experience for him.

Afterwards, Josh said, 'I think there are a few other skills that I would enjoy using if I was given the chance, like managing and overseeing others. Even though I was only there for a few weeks, I got a real buzz out of leading a team at Towers Media Group. I really liked the idea of making the most of everyone's contribution in the team.'

'Make a note of that then,' said Tomas. 'Some skills definitely emerge over time and as you find yourself in different situations.'

'One thing was running through my mind as I completed the questions. If it turns out that I have a number of strengths, which ones do I focus on leveraging or developing?' asked Josh.

'In my experience, if you're going to rise to the top of your field, then you need to focus on two or three areas and really excel in these. Otherwise, you'll just become a jack of all trades and master of none,' said Tomas.

Josh made a few notes.

'So what are you thinking of?' asked Tomas.

'Not sure. Customer services?' Josh said with a smirk.

'Well, I've never seen anyone fail in business who devotes his or her efforts to making the customer successful.'

'There you go,' said Josh. 'That was easy.'

'What about going into sales? It's quite a strong profile match,' said Tomas.

Josh shook his head. 'Sales? No way!'

'Have you ever tried it?'

'Not really, but salespeople are just thieves, and it's not my idea of helping people.'

'Don't you think that depends on what it is? I get the impression that you could really do well in a sales role if it was a product or service that you were really passionate about. It's worth considering.'

Josh was still gently shaking his head but said, 'Maybe.'

They talked for a little while longer before Josh had to leave.

***

The following week Josh had a job interview with Rupp Warr Linsey. Sonya had spoken to her husband who passed Josh's CV around. It was the first time he had spoken about himself during an interview with a clear understanding of his key strengths as a person. He was also much more confident talking about his areas for development.

When the recruitment consultant called back later that day, she told Josh that Rupp Warr Linsey wanted to meet Josh for a second interview. The original number of interviewees had been shortlisted from twenty to three.

Josh felt he was in with a good chance.

Summary of Principles and Lessons

All people have a unique contribution that they have to make to the world and a responsibility to find out what that is so they can make it.

A winning focus means discovering my top two or three strengths and doing everything I can to use those strengths as often as possible so that they develop, grow, and shine.

I'll be remembered for what I contributed rather than how I compared with others.

Having a passion for what I do is contagious. It's what will drive me to develop the skills I need to succeed. It's what will keep my spirit up even when the going is tough. It's what will compel me to put in the hard work and develop mastery, which in turn builds confidence.

To build on and leverage my strengths, I need to proactively seek feedback from those around me who can help me identify what I do well.

My strengths may also emerge through trial and error as I find myself drawn to things that I'm really good at.

Living out who I am, being the person I know I'm meant to be, is no mean feat. It always involves confronting my fears. And fear of failure is probably the biggest obstacle to overcome.

11—A New Era

I've come to believe that all my past failure and frustrations were actually laying the foundation for the understandings that have created the new level of living I now enjoy.

—Anthony Robbins

Tomas's house was easy to find. It was a large, detached house with a very long driveway. There were already a few cars parked outside, so Josh wasn't the first to arrive. Paul and Jaz couldn't make it because they were still away on their honeymoon. They had to delay it until Paul could get some good time off over the summer holiday.

Since Tomas couldn't make it to Paul's wedding, it had been almost eight months since Josh had seen him. Josh's new job meant that he had to do a lot of travelling. He couldn't believe how much he was enjoying his work. He'd never seen himself in sales, but it turned out he had more of a knack for it than he realised, especially when he believed in the product.

Although he didn't get the marketing job with the advertising firm Rupp Warr Linsey, the feedback he received after the second interview was his best ever. Shortly after that, several conversations with Tomas, Paul, and a few others made him realise that the only reason he didn't go into sales was because of his perception of the door-to-door salespeople who would come to his house as a child and sell loads of items that his family never needed and couldn't afford. That had tainted his view of selling.

However, from the feedback he received and his own reflections, he realised that he had always been a passionate communicator about things that he believed in. Also, the fact that he enjoyed working with people made him believe he would be motivated to serve rather than exploit his customers. Josh soon realised that his strengths meant it was very likely that he would excel in a sales role, so he decided to take the risk.

He also discovered that, rather than actually working with patients to diagnose and cure sicknesses, he was more excited about seeing the benefits people gained from medical advances and new technology. So when CJ offered to put him in touch with a friend who was a sales director for a medical technology firm that was owned by one of the largest pharmaceutical companies in the world, he jumped at the opportunity. After an initial conversation with the sales director, he was invited for a formal interview and took a personality test. At the interview, his experience in research and marketing turned out to be a huge advantage.

It had been a roller-coaster journey and an extremely tough time, financially, but Josh was excited about his new role as a sales executive and was committed to applying the key lessons he'd learnt from Tomas and the other executives since he first met them more than eighteen months ago.

As he got out of the car, a tall, well-dressed lady came out to meet him. 'You must be Josh,' she said.

'Yes, I am.' Josh had seen pictures of Tomas's family and knew this was Tomas's wife.

'Hi, I'm Jayne. Tomas's wife. He's told me quite a lot about you,' she said as they made their way into the house.

'I won't dare ask if it's all been good,' said Josh. 'However, I must say, he's been an amazing help to me.'

Jayne smiled.

'Thank you,' she said taking the wine and flowers Josh had brought.

She told Josh that Tomas was getting the barbeque going in the garden. He made his way to the garden to meet Tomas while Jayne continued with preparations for the party.

Almost three hours later, the birthday party for Tomas's ten-year-old son was in full swing. Some of the youngsters were running around in the garden, while others were having fun on the trampoline set up at the end of the garden. The adults were all sipping drinks and enjoying themselves.

'Taking the time to answer those questions helped steer me in the right direction,' said Josh as he spoke to Paula. Her son and Tomas's son were in the same school. 'At first, I thought I was going crazy when I turned down the offer to go back to work at Pete's firm. God knows I needed the money. But by that time, I realised that it just wasn't the right fit for me.'

'We've all done things because it's easier and simpler rather than because it's the best choice for us,' said Paula. 'We often choose the easier road and the path with least resistance rather than the path that brings about the greatest growth, challenge, and fulfilment.'

'That's exactly how I feel now. I've decided to choose the road less travelled, and I'm doing a lot of miles as a result.'

They both laughed.

'And you'll be all the better for it,' she assured him.

'One of the biggest challenges for me now is making sure that I have a good work-life balance. How do you all do it?'

By this time, they'd been joined by Sonya and her husband, Chris.

'Admittedly, that's a challenge,' said Paula. 'Some jobs aren't suited for good work-life balance. So I guess you need to weigh up the pros and cons and figure out what's important to you, especially as life changes. Personally, I've never had a work-life balance plan that was effective for more than six months. However, I do work that I love, and that makes all the difference. By other people's standards, I work harder and longer, but that's OK because it's work I love doing. What that means though is when I'm home, I can switch off. I very rarely take work home with me. I think it's very satisfying to work hard and give your best there and then give your best at home with family and friends. It also helps to keep a variety of interests outside work.'

Chris, Sonya's husband, jumped in. 'I like the way Woody Allen puts it: "Seize the opportunities, avoid the pitfalls, and be home by 6 p.m." Not that I've ever managed that. However, my family life has always mattered a great deal to me, so it's been a very strong counterweight to excessive work. I think a lot does depend on what you think about life. I've worked hard, but it's never been excessive. And I'm not just saying that because Sonya's here.'

They all chuckled.

'You've got to remember that you only live once, and there is more to life than work,' said Sonya.

'Yeah, you're right. It's just so easy to get caught up with work, especially when you're really enjoying it. It takes discipline to do otherwise,' said Josh.

'You bet it does,' Sonya replied. 'It's not easy, but that really depends on your core values and the core values of the people around you. If you're in an organisation that doesn't respect or value work-life balance, then it's going to be that much harder or you. But I think it does also depend on the stage of life you're at. I think your circumstances influence your work-life balance. As soon as I had a family, my work-life balance changed. Having children has certainly helped me have a good work-life balance. But I don't think there is such a thing as the ideal work-life balance; every individual has to figure it out for himself or herself.'

Jayne brought over some more drinks and food. 'Please tuck in. There's plenty,' she said.

'Try and stop me,' quipped Josh.

Summary of Principles and Lessons

We often choose the easier road and the path with least resistance rather than the path that brings about the greatest growth, challenge, and fulfilment.

Some jobs aren't suited for good work-life balance, so I need to count the cost and figure out what's important to me, especially as my life changes.

Doing work that I love can make a difference to my overall sense of work-life balance.

It's very satisfying to work hard and give my best there, and then give my best at home with family and friends.

Keep interests outside work.

Remember that I only live once—there is more to life than work.

There is no such thing as the ideal work-life balance; every individual has to figure it out for himself or herself.

Epilogue: Passing It On

We make a living by what we get,
but we make a life by what we give.

—Sir Winston Churchill

Eighteen months later, they were having a drink in the patisserie close to Tomas's office.

'It's a far cry from the recommendation I would have received when I first met you. Not that I was even thinking of this back then,' said Josh.

Tomas read the accolade from Josh's divisional director. It was part of a reference for his MBA.

> 'Josh is an exceptional and professional manager with strong commercial and leadership skills and a strong track record of delivering excellent customer service for our sales division. He has been a great asset to

our organisation and has built a reputation both within and outside for delivering on his promises. This comes from an ability to focus on activities that really make a difference to our overall company vision. He is always looking for ways to contribute and make improvements to our business as demonstrated by recently pioneering our involvement in youth development projects, which has in turn enhanced our reputation among our customers.'

'This is fantastic. So when do you start?' asked Tomas.

'Next year, and my company is giving me a full scholarship. One of the perks of being on the management fast-track scheme. I've also been asked to head up our new sales division in Paris. I'll be moving in a few months. It was a good thing I decided to pick up French again two years ago. I'm pushing to come to INSEAD, but there are no guarantees. I'm told the company prefers London Business School.'

'I'm sure that you'll get a lot out of it, whichever business school you go to.'

'What a journey it's been over the last three years. Sometimes, I still wish I had learnt some of those lessons sooner and not put myself through all the agony.'

'Very often, the only way to learn the lessons is to experience the agony.'

Josh nodded. 'Ah, yes, the butterfly and its growth pains.'

'There's no true transformation without pain and struggle. That's life! And what really matters now is that you have learnt the lessons and have also developed a hunger for continuous learning and growth. There are so many possibilities that will open up to you as you maintain the right attitude and focus.'

'I wouldn't have believed that when we first met, but now I do,' Josh replied. 'By the way, a few weeks ago, we had a retirement party for our outgoing CEO and some other long-serving staff members. I went along because two members of my team were retiring. Anyway, I asked the CEO and a few others if there was anything that they would do differently if they could turn back time. Some of them said things like taking more chances; seeing every experience, good or bad, as a learning opportunity; and being proactive.'

'Those are certainly great lessons to hold on to as you continue to develop in your career.'

'What would it be for you, Tomas, if anything?'

Tomas thought for a minute.

'You know what? I honestly feel great about the position that I'm in now, including all the experiences—failures and victories—that I've had. I'm richer for it.' He paused for a while and then said, 'However, there is one thing I would change, and that is to start building a life of significance a lot earlier.'

'What do you mean?'

'Well, like most ambitious people, I started off with the goal to be successful and be the best, but that had a lot to do with what I could acquire. Now, I've realised that it's more important that I commit to being my best because of what I can give to others. I love the work that I do. Yes, it is about building businesses and creating wealth, but the impact we're having on people's lives is what I find most rewarding. Ultimately, I think the human journey is about that—relationships. It's about people.'

'Giving wealth to others certainly does make a difference.'

'It's not just financial wealth but time, friendship, and mentoring.'

'You've got me thinking now. A life of significance ...'

Josh made a few notes and then quickly looked back up at Tomas. 'Speaking of mentoring,' said Josh, 'another thing that stood out when I asked that question was about seeking advice and mentoring early on. Until my experience with you and some of the others I met at the convention, I'd never really thought of or appreciated the value of mentoring.'

'A professor friend of mine always says, "If you want to know the condition of the road ahead, ask those who are coming back." That's how I view mentoring. It enables you to see more than you ever could on your own. It's an amazingly fast way of learning.'

'So would you say everyone should have at least one mentor then?' asked Josh.

'That's certainly the ideal situation,' Tomas said. 'But you do need to have the right attitude and approach in order to get the most out of it. Some people expect their mentor to make things happen for them. A mentor can certainly guide and even inspire you, but they can't live your life for you. Take us for example, when we first met I could've easily given you a job or asked someone I know to help, but I quickly realised that you needed to go on the journey that you did.'

'And I'm glad you let me go on that journey. So what tips do you give to anyone looking for a mentor?'

'I always say aim exceedingly high and approach them,' replied Tomas. 'Then capitalise on the opportunity. As with most things in life, you get out what you put in. That doesn't mean you should always take advice without testing it. I think the best mentees seek a number of mentors, not just one.'

'I guess it goes without saying that the mentee needs to take responsibility?'

'Yes, and manage their own expectations. However, I still think that mentoring is one of the most significant ways for an individual to develop personally and professionally. By the way, Josh, don't be afraid to offer a degree of mentoring yourself.'

'I'm not sure I have that much to offer just yet.'

'You already have more than you can realise.'

Josh smiled. 'OK. So what tips would you give me as a potential mentor then?'

Tomas paused for a minute and then said, 'I think a skilled mentor is someone who listens amazingly well and realises the value they bring to the mentee. Considering what I said earlier about living a life of significance, mentoring can be very rewarding because it's a way of giving inspiration and support to another individual and unlocking opportunities for them, directly or indirectly, through your own network.'

'I've certainly felt that, not just from you and the other executives I met at the convention but also from senior managers in my organisation. It's given me a very healthy and different perspective on my life and career.'

'That's already worth sharing with others,' Tomas offered.

'I guess so,' said Josh.

***

Two weeks later, Josh received a parcel. It was a book from Tomas on getting the most out of one's MBA. It also came with a handwritten note.

Dear Josh,

I'm very proud of how far you've come since we first met. The best mentoring relationships are always mutually beneficial. This was no exception.

Never lose your enthusiasm for learning and growing.

All the best,
TW

A few days later, Josh got in touch with the corporate HR department in his organisation and asked if he could be involved in mentoring. He was told that most of the mentors were senior managers but there was a review currently underway to engage more middle managers in the programme.

It wasn't long before Josh received confirmation that he could be a mentor on the internal mentoring programme. Tomas's comments rang true as he realised the rewards of supporting the development of others.

Later that year, after Josh had moved to Paris, he was named Intrapreneur of the Year. The Intrapreneur of the Year award was presented by the CEO to the divisional sales manager whose suggestions for business improvements had the greatest impact on the overall performance of the company.

As Intrapreneur of the Year, Josh delivered a short speech to the graduates and other recent recruits to his organisation at their annual one-day induction programme, which always featured corporate awards. After he was introduced, he walked to the platform and addressed the audience.

'Hi, everyone! A few months ago, a new member of my team mentioned that I almost always come into the office, even on a Monday, with a spring in my step and wanted to know what drives me. I quickly assured her that that wasn't always the case. You see, I used to think job satisfaction and success were mostly about things that were outside of me—my job, my boss, my environment, my salary, my colleagues, etc.

'But now I realise it has very little to do with any of those things and so much more to do with me. It's about becoming someone who people want to work with and want to hire. It's about discovering my passion and strengths and playing to those as best as I can to offer value to the organisation and the customers we serve. It's about bringing all my talents and creativity to the workplace. It's about being a person of value. I'm not talking about intrinsic worth, because I realise that we all have incredible potential and immeasurable worth, but what I mean is being someone who people know will diligently contribute in any environment despite the circumstances.

'If true success was all external—fast cars, big house, better boss, loads of money—then that would mean a majority of the world's population couldn't be successful. Luckily for me, thanks to some great mentors and friends over the years, I've realised that, ultimately, success is about the journey and giving my best along the way. I can't control outcomes. What I can do is choose my attitude and my actions.

'So now when I come to work, my attitude is to wholeheartedly and resolutely give the best of all that I have—my skills, my talents, my experiences, and my passion—right here, right now, because *that's when the magic really begins to happen.*'

***

A few weeks later, Josh called up Tomas to tell him that his company had decided on the London Business School instead of INSEAD.

'The good thing is that we can meet up on occasions when I'm in London, assuming you're in town and are free,' said Josh.

Josh went on to tell Tomas about his involvement in the mentoring scheme and the benefits he was seeing.

'That's why I'll never get tired of investing in the next generation,' said Tomas. 'I really believe there's so much potential in people just waiting to be released. I look at you, and I think it's worth it. Remember this: *things don't just happen.* They happen because you believe that they are going to happen and so you prepare yourself and do all that is within your power. Sometimes, you'll feel like a fraud, and then you'll realise you can actually do it. Don't be afraid to stand out. Be who you are, give the best of yourself to the world, and keep hold of that *winning attitude* and *winning focus.*'

Josh was silent for a while. 'I really don't know how to thank you for the last couple of years. It's almost like you've been a father to me. All I can say is that I feel compelled to somehow pass on to others all that I've learnt from you.'

'You certainly have an enriching story to tell. Remember, you can't actually make people get it; they've got to get it for themselves.'

'Let's just say I'm willing to do whatever it takes to persuade them.'

'How about write a book?' asked Tomas.

'Er … Almost anything.'

They both chuckled.

About the Author

Obi Abuchi founded Motivatem in 2008 as a consultancy to help organisations improve performance by effectively tapping into and releasing the full potential and motivation of their employees. He is a chartered member of the Chartered Institute of Personnel and Development (CIPD), the world's largest chartered HR and development professional body.

Prior to setting up Motivatem, Obi began his career as an engineer, having achieved a bachelor's and master's degree in manufacturing systems engineering with management from King's College London. Upon graduation, he joined Metronet Rail, an engineering and construction organisation with responsibility for a multi-billion-pound schedule of improvement and maintenance of the London Underground. During his time with Metronet Rail he gained experience in business change projects before joining FBM Consulting, a London-based business and change management consultancy as a senior consultant in 2006.

He has worked with private and public sector organisations in the UK, Channel Islands, and Europe, including Shell, EDF Energy, and Northern Ireland Water, as well as third sector organisations, integrating business, HR, organisational development, and talent strategies to create value through people.

Obi also channels his combined experience to facilitate peak performance and excellence in young people and young professionals. He co-founded the Young Talent Network in 2008, which has partnered with blue chip companies such as Bank of America Merrill Lynch, British Petroleum (BP), British Telecom (BT), Deloitte, and Ernst and Young to deliver career insight programmes.

He has served as a business mentor at his alma mater, delivered enterprise and training programmes in schools and colleges across the UK and Channel Islands, and has been a guest speaker at international conferences in London and Washington, DC, speaking to groups of more than 750 people on topics such as 'the importance of empowering young people,' 'achievement,' and 'single-mindedness toward achieving our goals.'

His passion for making a difference has also seen him get involved in community-based charity projects in the UK, USA, Central America, and Jamaica.

Obi, his wife, Peju, and their three sons live in London, England.

Helping Organisations Win!

Dictionary Definition of Attitude - *"A settled way of thinking or feeling, typically reflected in a person's behaviour."*

Winning Attitude - *"A positive state of mind or way of thinking that empowers you to wholeheartedly and resolutely do whatever it takes to give the BEST of who you are—skills, talents, experience, and passion—to your family, life, and work."* —*Obi Abuchi*

Whether they define it as an increase in turnover, performance, market share, profit, or talent retention, every organisation wants to win. Winning, of course, begins with a state of mind that determines the right beliefs: *I can win*; which determines the right expectations: *I will win*; which determines the right attitude: *I am going to develop a plan to win*; which determines the right behaviours: *I've developed the plan and will do whatever it takes to follow through*; which determines the right performance and the desired results: *I won!*

Obi's keynote talks and seminars are designed to inspire, engage, and motivate your staff to develop a winning attitude and increase their overall performance and productivity.

Winning F.A.S.T.E.R.™

Delegates learn powerful ideas, techniques, and strategies to enable them increase their productivity, performance, and contribution to their organisations goals by focusing on six critical areas:

- A Winning *F*ocus *(leveraging their unique strengths and capabilities)*
- Winning *A*ttitude
- Winning *S*elf-Discipline
- Winning *T*ime Management Practices
- A Winning *E*xposure Strategy
- Winning *R*esilience

Breaking Through Fear

Fear of failure, or fear of rejection (e.g., in sales), or even fear of success stops many professionals from maximising their full potential in achieving their personal and professional goals. World-class athletes and professionals are not super-humans with no fears, they have simply developed strategies to enable them overcome their fears and do what needs to be done. Learn seven powerful and effective strategies (C.O.U.R.A.G.E.) for breaking through fear.

Visit www.motivatem.co.uk or call on 0207 712 1670 for more information or booking availability.

Discover Your Sphere of Excellence™

Your sphere of excellence is that arena where your talents, passions, skills, education, experience, and unique personality merge together with empowering beliefs, based on the right expectations, to create a powerful combination that unleashes your unique potential.

—*Obi Abuchi*

Are you performing at your best?

Do you know what you can be great at?

Do you know your top skills and talents and how to hone them?

Far too many people miss the magical opportunity to invest their passions and strengths to drive business results and excel in their career or chosen vocation. Inevitably, this leads to reduced productivity, greater levels of stress and worry, and a general sense of dissatisfaction and lack of fulfilment in their lives. Yet, the truth is, most people would love to go to work feeling energised, empowered, and engaged because they are doing what they do best and are flourishing in their career!

That's exactly what happens when you discover *Your Sphere of Excellence*™. It's that arena where people look at you and say, 'They make it look *so* easy!' The great news is that *everybody* has his or her own unique sphere of excellence. The challenge, as is often the case, is discovering it with certainty and clarity. However, if you want to

- get more done with ease;
- accomplish more with confidence;
- increase your productivity and reduce stress;
- focus on the things that really do make a difference to your organization; and
- excel in your career,

Then it's important—no, *essential*—that you discover **Your Sphere of Excellence**™ and so begin performing at your best!

Motivatem's **Your Sphere of Excellence**™ coaching and training programme teaches effective strategies and techniques for

- discovering your strengths and passions and utilising them in your daily working life to increase your performance and productivity;
- developing empowering beliefs and overcoming limiting fears, doubts, and insecurities;
- positively impacting your career now and in the future;
- developing and utilising your top talents; and
- honing your top skills.

Visit www.motivatem.co.uk or call on 0207 712 1670 for more information.